Motorcycling Manual

Motorcycling Manual

By the Staff of
'Motorcycling Monthly'

Compiled by John Thorpe

Hamlyn
London · New York · Sydney · Toronto

Published by The Hamlyn Publishing Group Limited
London · New York · Sydney · Toronto
Astronaut House, Feltham, Middlesex, England

Third Impression 1981

ISBN 0 600 36301 5

Printed in Italy

Contents

A Multitude of motorcycles

This is the true Golden Age of motor cycling. The range of bikes now on the market comprises every conceivable type – but they all have one thing in common. Unlike the undemanding machines of earlier days, modern bikes require the highest standards of maintenance and overhaul work. Clearances can be critical to fractions of a millimetre: settings to minutes, rather than degrees. Power, smoothness and reliability are there: but they have to be paid for in meticulous attention to detail. That demands, in turn, a full understanding of the characteristics of each engine layout and each chassis.

Apart from the few Wankel-engined bikes that have been produced by a small minority of factories, all current machines have either two-stroke or four-stroke piston engines. This, at least, is something that is unlikely to change radically. Emission-control regulations, however, mean increasingly that the mechanically-simpler two-stroke engine is being replaced by the more complicated four-stroke. This extra complication is real. A twin-cylinder two-stroke engine, for example, has just seven moving parts. A four-cylinder four-stroke giving identical firing intervals, has over 40.

Typical engine layouts

Two-strokes: singles. – One of the favourite configurations for low-powered utility bikes, the simplest two-stroke engine comprises a single cylinder, with piston-controlled ports for gas flow. It has a single carburettor, feeding a mixture of petrol and oil first into the crankcase via an inlet port, then through transfer ports into the cylinder. The underside of the piston is used as a pump for this purpose. After the mixture has been fired by a single sparking plug set in the cylinder head, the residue is exhausted through a further port cut in the base of the cylinder. All ports are opened and closed solely by movement of the piston.

Such an engine needs only three moving parts: crankshaft; connecting rod; piston. Lubrication is achieved by the admixture of oil with the petrol. Power units of this type are almost invariably air cooled. The sizes range from mopeds of 50 cc and under, up to quite sporting 250 cc motorcycles. A few larger engines have been produced in the past, but efficiency is low if the capacity is increased much beyond the 250 cc limit.

Greater power and more economical operation can be obtained by controlling the entry of the fuel mixture by means of a disc valve or a reed valve. This allows a longer period of induction; impossible with the piston-controlled port, through which mixture can be driven out again as the piston descends.

Lubrication can also be im-

Sporty '50' – the Honda SS50, with near-horizontal four-stroke engine

proved by use of a separate oil pump. This is normally linked to the throttle control, so that the amount of oil injected by the pump is proportionate to the engine speed and load.

Two-strokes: twins. – These can be regarded virtually as two single-cylinder engines coupled together, with their cranks arranged at 180° to each other. With this arrangement, the cylinders are in parallel, and the pistons rise and fall alternately. Since a two-stroke engine has one firing stroke to each revolution of the crankshaft, the firing intervals of the two-stroke twin are identical with those of the four-stroke 'four', and the balance is similar to that of the uneven-firing 180° four-stroke twin.

Twin two-strokes can be simple 'piston-port' motors with petroil lubrication: or sophisticated units with disc or reed valve induction, and pump lubrication. Normally air cooled – although water-cooled versions have been made – they can range from 100 cc to 700 cc capacity.

Two-strokes: triples. – Three two-stroke cylinders set side by side, with cranks arranged at 120° to each other, give the same firing intervals as a six-cylinder four-stroke. Early motors of this type suffered severe cooling problems, but water-cooling has been adopted in only a few cases. Current triples usually have some form of valve controlling the induction, and employ forced lubrication. Transistorised ignition systems are also used on some motors, where the job of supplying up to 30,000

A dual-purpose bike – Suzuki's TS185 combines rough-riding capability with economical daily transport

sparks every minute on the higher-performance units proved to be beyond the capabilities of conventional contact-breakers. The smallest triples fall into the 350–400 cc category: the largest, generally speaking, are around 750 cc. Fuel consumption can be uneconomically high, but the power output from a well-tuned big triple – applied to a fairly light bike – is often thought to compensate for it.

Four-strokes: singles. – At one time the dominant type of motorcycle power unit, the single-cylinder four-stroke suffered a near-eclipse in the early 1970s, but seems certain to make a comeback in the closing years of the decade. Invariably air cooled, single-cylinder four-strokes normally use overhead-valve operation. For both simplicity and efficiency, an overhead camshaft mounted in the cylinder head can be used to operate the valves. A few machines, however, retain push-rod valve operation. Here, the camshaft is mounted in the crankcase, and the cams bear on followers in which the push-rod feet are set. The upper end of each of the rods bears on one side of a rocker, pivoted at its mid point. The other end of the rocker depresses the valve when the cam presses the push rod upwards. Valve closure is normally effected by springs, but in desmodromic designs – invariably overhead camshaft units – valve closure is made positive by a second set of rockers and fingers. Supplementary valve springs are sometimes incorporated in the system.

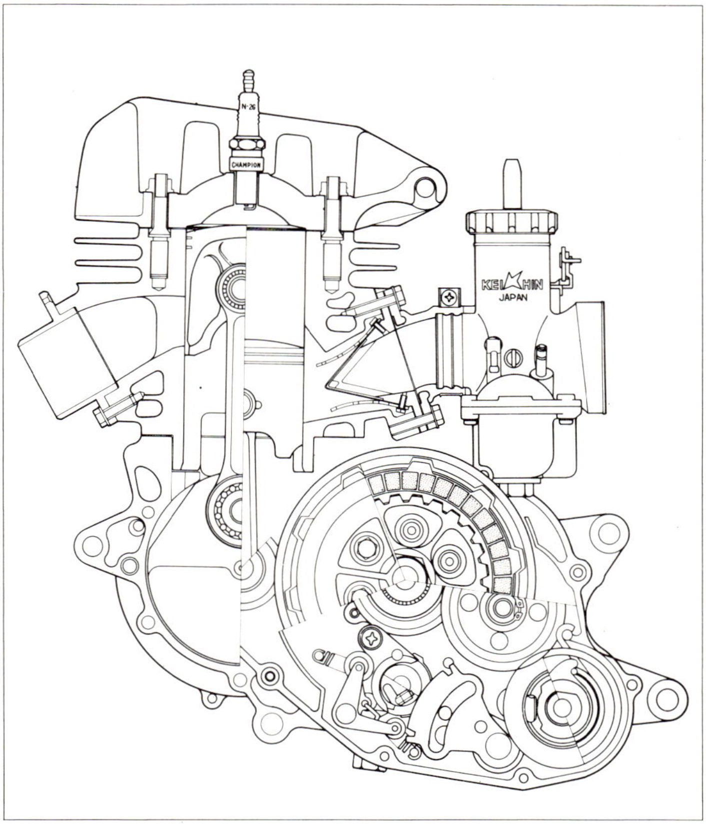

By comparison with a four-stroke, a two-stroke is simplicity itself. This is a peppy sports engine – Honda's CR250R, used on works moto-cross bikes. Despite its great power, it has just three basic moving parts – piston, connecting rod, and crankshaft. One of the secrets is the reed valve, seen here in the inlet port. This opens to allow mixture to enter the crankcase, but closes to prevent blow-back as the piston descends

Alternative four-stroke valve layouts are side-valves – where the valves are mounted alongside the cylinder, and open upwards into a side extension of the cylinder head; inlet-over-exhaust, where one valve is side-mounted and the other is set in the head; rotary – used only in a few largely-unsuccessful pre-war units; and sleeve, in which ports are cut in a movable cylinder liner – a type found only on rare vintage engines.

All four-strokes employ positive lubrication from a pump. The almost universal system in current use is to feed oil under pressure from a separate tank, or from a sump, to all areas of high loading – eg, big-end and small-end bearings; main bearings; valve gear; etc. – and to return it to the tank for re-circulation. In the process, it is passed through a filter which removes impurities. Frequently, the transmission gears are partly immersed in the main oil supply, and Japanese practice often includes forced lubrication of high-stress areas in the transmission.

Four-strokes: parallel twins. – Basically, two four-stroke cylinders set side by side, and mounted vertically, inclined, or flat. The crankpins may be in line with each other (set at 360°) or arranged so that when one is at TDC the other is at BDC (set at 180°). In the first case, the balance is little better than with a single-cylinder engine, but the firing intervals are evenly spaced. Units of this type fire once on each revolution of the crankshaft.

With 180° twins, the mechanical

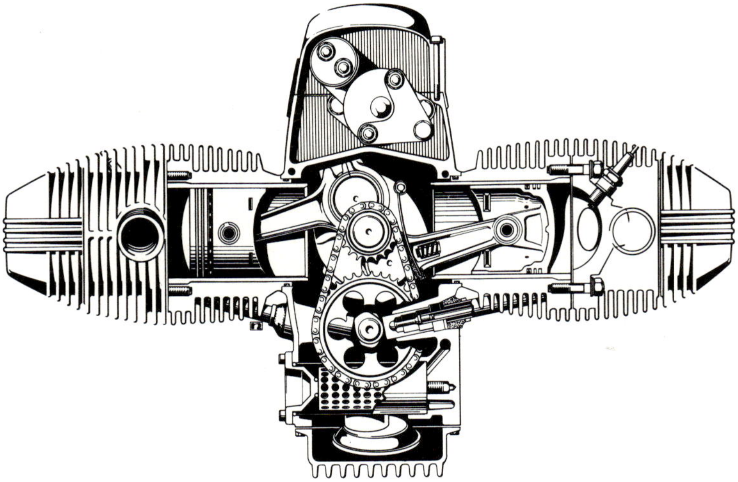

The basis of the four-stroke engine is represented by this cutaway view of the bottom end of the flat-twin BMW engine. Each piston is mounted on its own crankpin on the crankshaft, and in this case they move inwards and outwards together. This gives perfect balance and even firing. A parallel-twin is basically a flat-twin which has been 'folded up' so that the cylinders are vertical. With the same 180° crankshaft, balance would remain good, but the cylinders would fire on successive strokes. For this reason, many parallel-twins use a 360° crankshaft with the pistons rising and falling together. The balance – about the same as that of a single-cylinder engine – can be improved by use of balance shafts, and even firing intervals are then retained

Opposite, lower: only a twin-cylinder engine – but still a mass of machinery! The CX500 power unit includes the engine and gearbox in one compact mass, which aids the bike's handling. To balance out the rotating mass of the crankshaft and flywheel, the clutch is arranged to turn in the opposite direction. This successfully overcomes the tendency to twitch which has been a fault with many earlier shaft-drive bikes

balance is superior to that of the single or the 360° twin, but the firing intervals are uneven.

Four-strokes: horizontally-opposed twins. – Apart from a rocking couple resulting from the need to offset the centre lines of the cylinders, the flat twin – one in which the cylinders are placed on opposite sides of the crankcase – offers perfect balance and even firing. When set transversely, as in the BMW, cooling is no problem, but there is sometimes a reluctance to accept the layout through fear of the cylinders being damaged in a spill. Pre-war machines often had the unit mounted with the cylinders fore and aft, but this posed cooling problems, and dictated an awkward transmission layout.

The modern solution is to set the engine transversely – ideal for shaft drive – and to keep the engine width within acceptable limits by using a relatively short stroke and large bores.

All current flat twins have push-rod operated overhead valves and air cooling, although the LE Velocette which was still in production until a few years ago had side valves and water cooling.

Four-strokes: Vee-twins. – For many years the most popular type of twin-cylinder engine, the Vee-twin fell largely into dis-use save in the USA. It is now making a come-back.

The cylinders are set at an angle to each other – 45°, 72°, 80° and 90° are typical arrangements, although up to 120° has been used in the past – and the connecting rods are usually coupled to a single crankpin. This arrangement gives quite reasonable balance, uneven firing, and a rocking couple – but the units can be notably smooth-running.

Even firing can be arranged by off-setting the crankpins, but balance then suffers. It is usual for the cylinders to be offset one to another – or for the connecting-rod eyes to be asymmetric – to allow the rods to be mounted side by side on a single crankpin. Air cooling is normal, but the transversely-mounted Honda CX500 is liquid cooled.

Four-strokes: triples. – Usually mounted with the crankshaft across the frame, the four-stroke triple has crankpins set at 120° to give excellent balance – as with the Vee-twin, the pistons are never in phase with each other – at the cost of an uneven firing pattern.

Four-strokes: in-line fours. –

The Kawasaki KL250 trail bike. The motor is basically similar to its 200 cc touring stablemate, but with extra capacity and power. And the bike is designed to tackle really rough going off the beaten track, with high ground clearance and a fixed front mudguard that cannot clog with mud on wet ground

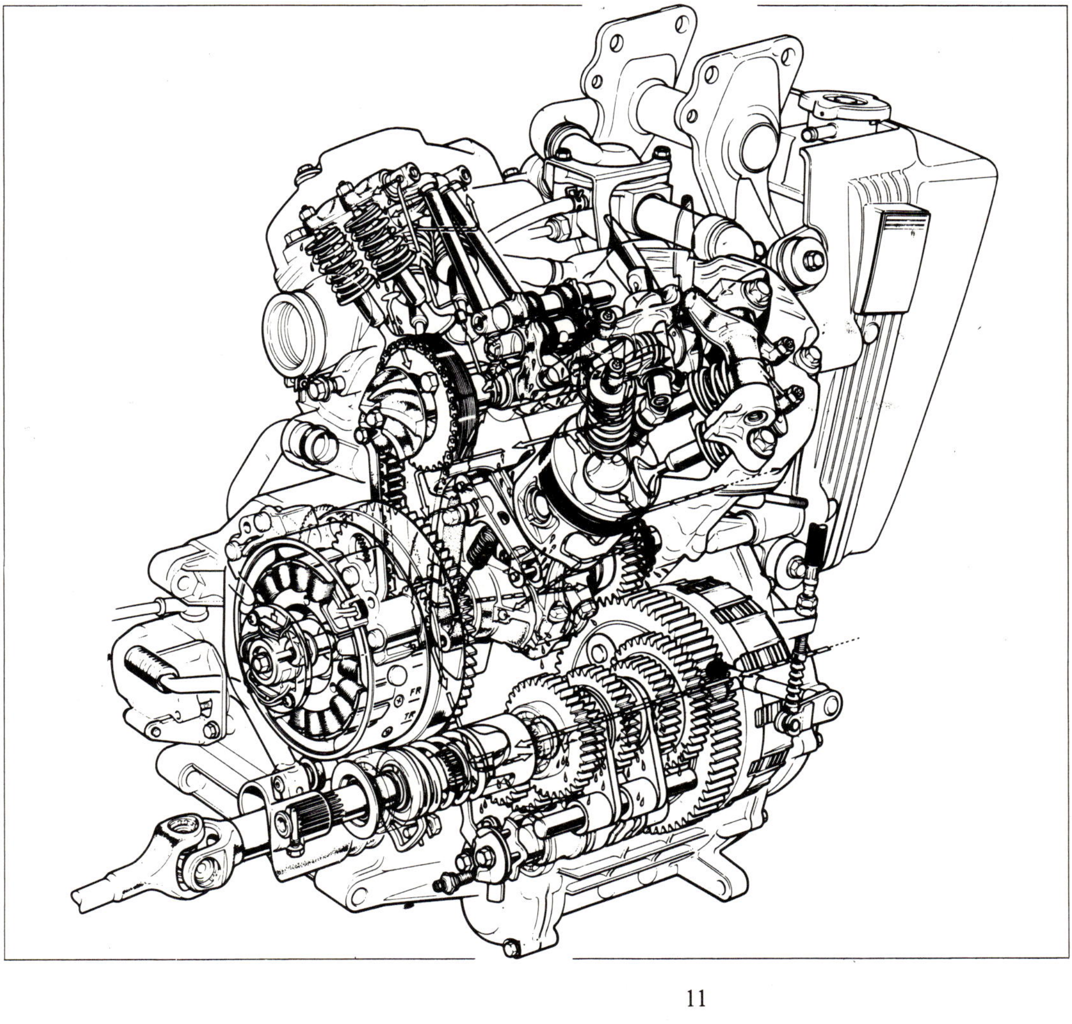

A simple commuter single with a sports performance, the Kawasaki Z200 has a single ohc all-alloy engine, typical of current practice in this field

Now the most popular type of four-cylinder engine, the in-line four is normally set transversely and is air cooled. Overhead camshaft operation of the valves is universal, with double ohc aplications gaining ground. The balance of a four-cylinder engine is good, and the firing intervals absolutely even, with two power strokes to each revolution of the crankshaft. Older applications of the in-line unit – motorcycles of this type have been produced for more than 70 years – often failed through overheating, due to the unit being set along the frame rather than across it. This also produced handling problems. One successful variation was the square engine, which was basically two 180° parallel-twin motors mounted in tandem, with their cranks geared.

Four-strokes: horizontally-opposed fours. – Combining near-perfect balance with even firing and reasonable dimensions, the flat-four engine is probably the ideal motorcycle power unit. Oddly, however, only Honda among the major producers has so far made a success of it in production. Unlike most previous flat-four designs, their ohc 'Gold Wing' has water cooling – dictated, in part, as much by the decision to use a toothed-belt camshaft drive as by the need to achieve constant running temperatures.

Four-strokes: Vee-fours. – Me-

chanically, a Vee-four can be regarded as two Vee-twins coupled to a common crankshaft. It is more compact than a flat-four and allows greater flexibility in design, since there is ample ground clearance when the machine is banked. The relatively poor mechanical balance can be offset by use of a counter-balance shaft.

Four-strokes: in-line sixes. – Perfect balance and near-ideal firing intervals make the in-line six a super-smooth engine, but mechanically complicated. The long crankshaft needed for a six also tends to be torsionally weak, and very careful engineering is needed in its production.

Four-strokes: Vee-sixes. – Although not as smooth as an in-line six, the Vee-six unit is more compact and has a more rigid bottom end assembly. Its inherent imbalance – as with a Vee-four – can be damped out by a counter-balance shaft.

Rotary-piston engines. – Normally called 'Wankel' engines, after their inventor, rotary-piston engines have generally failed to live up to their promise, and very few motorcycle power units of this type are now made. Their great advantage is simplicity: the moving parts are basically just the trichoid rotor-piston and its shaft. Although the operation is basically that of a four-stroke, there are no valves – just ports opened and closed by the rotor, rather like a two-stroke.

Final development of a machine that set the style for a generation of superbikes – the F2 version of the immortal Honda CB750. This transverse ohc four first appeared late in the 1960s. It has been refined into this ultimate sports version – fast and handy enough to have been used by the travelling marshals in the TT races

Strong men wept when this bike went out of production! The Triumph Trident – a 750 – was one of the first successful four-stroke triples. Bikers who own them are fanatical about the type

The ultimate in sporting Vee-twins – the 750 cc Moto Guzzi Le Mans combines a shattering performance with handling that recalls the factory's long history of successful racing machine development

Another factory that has a history of specialisation. Most Harley-Davidsons built since 1903 have been Vee-twins. The FX1200 typifies the Harley layout – big 45° Vee motor, with push-rod operated valves, set in a stiff frame, and still with a separate gearbox

One of the fastest bikes in its class, the Suzuki GS550 is a double-ohc 'four'

BMWs have used the flat twin engine since 1923 – and all have had shaft drive too. Typical of modern BMW practice, this 900 cc model was regarded as one of the best ever built

Above: the Honda GL1000 Gold Wing. This has a horizontally-opposed four-cylinder engine, with belt-driven overhead camshafts and liquid cooling. A counter-rotating alternator cancels out crankshaft torque reaction, and a fuel pump lifts the fuel from a low-set tank concealed beneath the saddle. The conventional-looking saddle tank is a 'dummy' that conceals the electrics, air filters, tool kit, and header tank for the coolant. As with the BMW, shaft drive is used

Cast light-alloy wheels that obviate wire spokes – difficult to keep in tension with modern bike power outputs – are a feature of the Suzuki GS1000. The twin overhead camshafts have bucket tappets, and each of the four cylinders is fed by its own carburettor

Above: the bottom-end assembly of Yamaha's successful 750 cc four-stroke triple – the XS750. The crank has pins set at 120°, giving good engine balance and constant torque. The power produced can be judged by the size of the Hy-Vo chain that is used to transmit it from the crankshaft to the clutch

Perhaps the definitive superbike – this time, Honda's answer to the quest for performance. This is the 1,047 cc double-ohc six-cylinder CBX, with Comstar wheels in which alloy rims are married to stainless-steel 'spokes'. Such a machine puts into the hands of a road rider the sort of power – around 100 bhp – that has previously been the preserve only of racers

Engines

Even the most potent of today's superbikes has an engine that would, at basis, have been familiar enough to the steam engineers of the early 1800s! The basic components of a piston engine – piston, cylinder, connecting rod, crankshaft, and crankcase – still remain in general use today, even though in a highly sophisticated form.

Every internal combustion engine – with the exception of the trochoid-piston Wankel, or the fully-rotary gas turbine – uses these basic components.

At the heart of the engine lies the cycle of operations – either two-stroke or four-stroke. Today, it is the four-stroke unit that is the most popular, and one that is growing in appeal as anti-pollution regulations begin to bite.

Four-stroke cycle

At its simplest, a four-stroke engine consists of a piston sliding in a cylinder closed, at one end, by a head and at the other by a crankcase. The head is equipped with an inlet and an exhaust valve, opened in a predetermined sequence by a cam.

The piston is linked, by a connecting rod, to a crankshaft carried in the crankcase. One of the main shafts that are part of the crankshaft drives a gear train or chain controlling the camshaft. Another transmits the power produced by the engine.

To provide a mixture capable of being burned in the cylinder, the unit is equipped with a carburettor. This is basically a device that takes liquid petrol and air, and which breaks down the petrol into droplets capable of mixing with air in a ratio of roughly one part petrol to fourteen of air by weight. It also has a throttle valve to control the admission of the mixture to the cylinder.

To fire the mixture, the cylinder head is fitted with a sparking plug. This comprises two electrodes, one fully insulated, and the other earthed. There is a small gap between them, and a high-tension current fed into the insulated electrode jumps the gap in the form of a hot blue spark. Correctly timed, this ignites the mixture in the cylinder, which has previously been compressed into a space of perhaps a tenth of its original volume. Its expansion drives the piston, which turns the crank, and so drives the motorcycle.

With a four-stroke engine, there are four phases (strokes) to this cycle of operations. It starts with the piston at the top of the cylinder, with the inlet valve open and the exhaust valve closed. A piston in this position is said to be at 'top dead centre' – usually abbreviated to TDC.

When the crankshaft is turned, the crankpin on the crankshaft draws the connecting rod down, pulling the piston with it. The effect is to increase the volume within the cylinder, and so lower the internal pressure below that

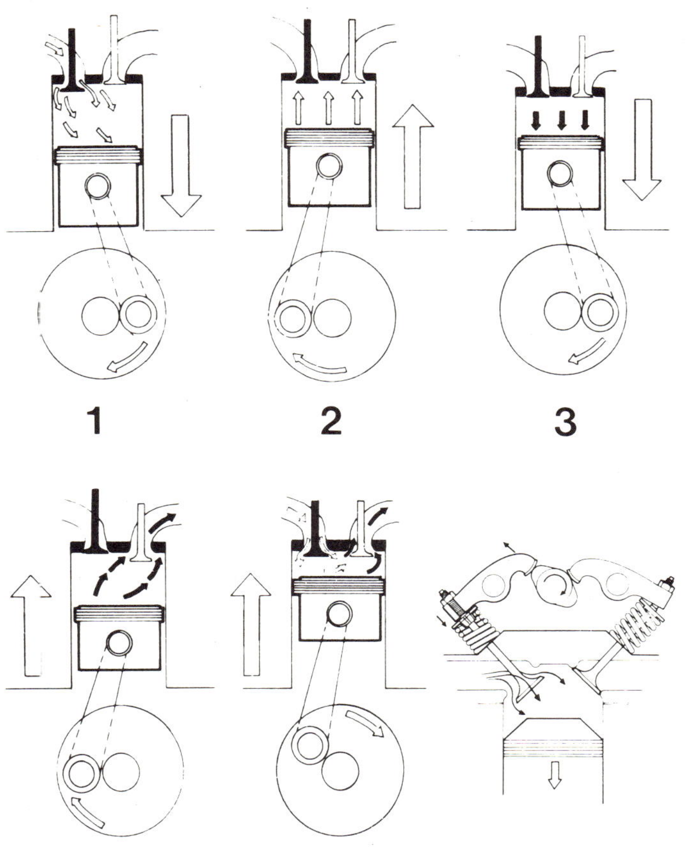

How it Works – Four-strokes
1. The crankshaft turns clockwise, and the connecting rod pulls the piston down. This lowers the pressure in the cylinder. The cam opens the inlet valve, and mixture is pushed in by atmospheric pressure. This is the induction stroke.
2. As the spinning flywheel causes the connecting rod to push the piston back up the cylinder bore both valves are closed, and the trapped mixture is compressed into perhaps one tenth of its volume. This is the compression stroke.
3. As the piston reaches its uppermost point of travel, a spark ignites the mixture. It burns rapidly, and in doing so expands. Its pressure forces the piston down the cylinder, so driving the flywheel. This is the power stroke.
4. Again, the spinning flywheel causes the piston to be thrust up the cylinder. This time, the exhaust valve is opened, and the piston pushes out the burned gases. This is the exhaust stroke.
5. There is a short period at the end of the exhaust stroke and the beginning of the induction stroke when both valves are open. This is called valve 'overlap'. It allows the movement of the exhaust gas to start drawing in the new mixture, so that the cycle can begin again.
6. Actual operation of the valves is by pressing them from their seats, against the resistance of their springs. The most common method today is to use a camshaft set in the cylinder head, operating the valves through rockers

of the atmosphere. The outside air therefore rushes through the carburettor, and is mixed with fuel on the way. It continues to enter the cylinder until the piston reaches the lower end of its travel (bottom dead centre: known as BDC), when the inlet valve is closed. This movement of the piston from TDC to BDC, with the inlet valve open, is known as the induction stroke: one stroke being the travel of a piston from TDC to BDC, or from BDC to TDC.

In revolving, the crankshaft has built up a momentum. Instead of stopping at the end of the induction stroke, it rises up the cylinder. The inlet valve has closed: the exhaust valve has yet to open. With both valves tightly shut, therefore, the rising piston compresses the trapped petrol/air mixture until, at TDC, all the mixture is trapped in the space between the top of the piston (its 'crown') and the head. This is known as the combustion chamber; the stroke during which compression takes place is the compression stroke. (The compression ratio is the ratio of the sum of the cylinder and combustion chamber volumes to the combustion chamber volume.)

So far, two complete strokes have been made and the crankshaft has turned once, yet no power has been produced. That is now rectified: because a spark is made to jump across the sparking plug points, igniting the mixture trapped in the combustion chamber.

The result is dramatic. A flame-front spreads rapidly through the chamber as the petrol/air mixture catches fire. As it burns, the heat causes rapid expansion of the compressed gas, and this presses hard on all the surrounding surfaces. Of these, only one can move – the piston. The effect is to thrust the piston down the cylinder – hard. As it descends, it presses down the connecting rod, which in turn swings the crankpin, and powers round the crankshaft. This is called the power stroke.

By the end of the power stroke, the energy of the gases is spent, and the residue needs to be ejected from the cylinder. Again, the momentum of the crankshaft, or its flywheel, makes the piston rise up the cylinder. As it does so, the exhaust valve is opened, and the burned gas is driven out ahead of the rising piston. This is the exhaust stroke.

As the piston approaches TDC, the inlet valve again opens. With the piston again at TDC, the cycle of operations has been completed – induction, compression, power, exhaust. The crankshaft has turned twice in this cycle, and only one stroke in four has been a power stroke.

Two-stroke cycle

That, in essence, is the four-stroke cycle. However, engineers have been able to telescope these four strokes into two, and so gain a power stroke to each revolution of the crankshaft. The result is the two-stroke engine, in which the valves of the four-stroke are replaced by holes (ports) cut in the cylinder walls, opened and closed by movement of the piston.

The two-stroke has the advantage of being simpler than the four-stroke, and in recent years has been at least its equal in power. Here is how it works.

We still have the basic engine – piston, connecting rod, crankshaft, and crankcase. An essential difference, however, is that the crankcase is made gas-tight, and the carburettor is connected to it. The cylinder head, too, is plain – it has no valves.

Imagine that a charge of gas has

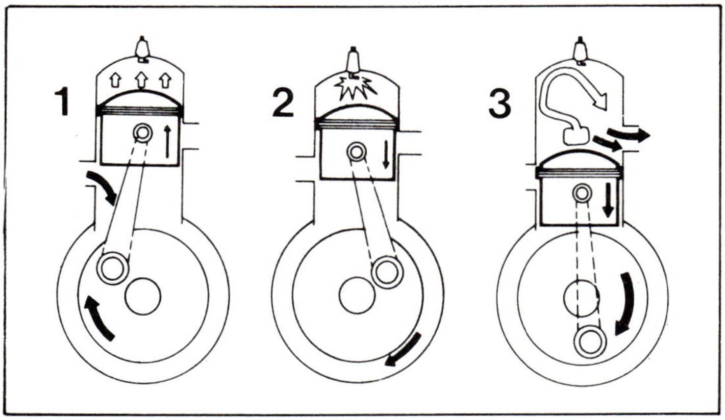

How it Works – Two-strokes
1. The two-stroke has a piston, cylinder, connecting rod and flywheel – but no four-stroke type valves. Instead, on the intake and cylinder compression stroke the fresh mixture is drawn into the crankcase under the piston, while the previous charge is being compressed in the cylinder.
2. As with the four-stroke, the mixture in the cylinder is ignited by a spark. It burns, and drives down the piston. The underside of the piston therefore compresses the gas trapped in the crankcase, since the piston's lower edge shuts off the inlet port through which it entered as the piston travels down the cylinder.
3. Approaching the bottom of its stroke, the piston uncovers an exhaust port, and the burned gases rush out. A moment later, it uncovers a pair of transfer ports connecting the crankcase to the cylinder. It pumps the fresh mixture out of the crankcase and into the cylinder, the ports being angled so that the streams collide and shoot upwards, away from the open exhaust port. Further piston movement closes the transfer ports, then the exhaust port. Lastly, its skirt opens the inlet port, while the top of the piston is compressing the mixture in the cylinder, and the cycle is complete

been drawn into the cylinder, compressed, and is about to be ignited with the piston at TDC. While the piston crown has been compressing the charge previously drawn in, the other end of the piston (the skirt) has uncovered a port connecting the carburettor to the crankcase. Upwards movement of the piston has increased the volume of the crankcase, and so lowered the internal pressure. Therefore, as soon as the piston uncovers the port (the inlet port, in this case) atmospheric pressure forces fuel/air mixture into the casing.

At the top of the engine, inside the combustion chamber, the previous charge is ignited. As in the four-stroke, it expands, and thrusts the piston down the cylinder. At once, the descending piston's lower edge closes the inlet port, trapping the mixture in the crankcase. Further movement of the piston compresses this trapped mixture.

Towards the end of its downward stroke, the top of the piston begins to uncover another port, cut in the wall of the cylinder. This is the exhaust port, and as it begins to open the still-expanding gas in the cylinder rushes out through it, impelled by its own inertia.

A fraction of a second later, the crown of the piston uncovers another port (or, more usually, a pair of ports) which connect the cylinder to the crankcase. These are the transfer ports, through which the partly-compressed new charge in the crankcase is pumped by the underside of the piston straight into the cylinder. The ports are angled towards each other, so that the two gas streams impinge, and are deflected up towards the head, away from the exhaust port. This is important, since the exhaust port, having opened first, has to close last, and unless the transferred gas streams were diverted too much of the new charge would be pumped straight into the exhaust pipe.

Now the still-revolving crankshaft moves the piston upwards again. As it travels up the cylinder, its upper edge first closes the transfer ports, then the exhaust port. Now the mixture trapped in the cylinder begins to be compressed. As the piston nears TDC, its lower edge uncovers the inlet port, and a new charge is induced into the crankcase, ready to be transferred on the next power stroke.

The two-stroke cycle is then complete. It has consisted of a power stroke in the cylinder which was combined with a compression stroke in the crankcase; and a compression stroke in the cylinder combined with what is effectively an induction stroke in the crankcase. In addition, part of the cylinder's power stroke has been utilised for an exhaust phase; and there has been an almost concurrent transfer phase.

Cooling system

Basic engines comprising little more than the bare components already mentioned have worked – although not very well and not for very long! To be practical, a motor needs to be rather more refined. We have already noted that a motorcycle engine works, basically, by converting heat into energy. Much of this heat is left unused and, in addition, the friction between the moving parts generates local heat; all this unusable heat has to be removed.

Part of this heat is dissipated by the engine cooling system; the rest by the lubrication system. Either can be extremely simple, or very sophisticated – and modern motorcycle engineering includes examples of both.

The simplest method is air cooling. Here, the unit is cooled through fins formed on the cylinder and cylinder head. These increase the surface area exposed to the surrounding air, so that the heat that is absorbed by the engine is radiated into the airflow as the motorcycle moves. It is simple, cheap, and effective – effective enough to be usable even on big 1,000 cc superbike multis, although manufacturing the complex castings gives production engineers a few headaches.

In general, air-cooled engines tend to run hotter than the ideal operating temperature, and in some instances could become overheated if kept running too long at a standstill. Engine enclosure, as on a scooter or behind a fairing, can be a problem too. The generally adopted answer for scooters is to use forced-air cooling, in which air is pumped through a trunking enclosing the barrel and head, a fan being formed on the flywheel for the purpose. In practice, the system works well, the only snag being that driving the fan absorbs an increasingly-large share of the engine's power the faster the motor turns. Faired-in motorcycle engines have to rely on what cooling they can get!

The obvious alternative to air cooling is liquid cooling. Here, the cylinder is surrounded by a jacket and the head has internal passages that link with it. The jacket is filled with a water/anti-freeze mixture.

As the engine heats up, so does the coolant. To keep the temperature even, the coolant is pumped to a radiator – basically, a labyrinth of pipes interspersed with cooling fins – in which the excess heat is radiated to the airflow. Thence, it returns to the cylinder jackets.

Pump operation is normal for current water-cooling systems, although a thermo-syphon system – in which the water circulates by rising as it heats and sinking as it

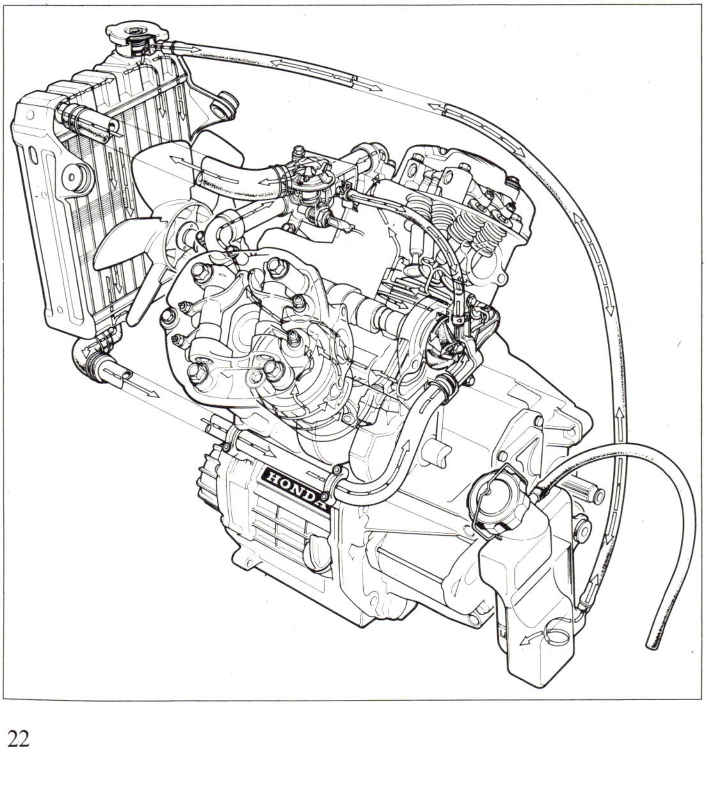

Most engines are still air cooled, relying on the slipstream to dissipate the heat from the motor as it passes over fins on the head and barrel. Liquid cooling, however, has considerable advantages, and the CX500 Honda illustrates modern thinking on the subject. Water is circulated by a pump driven off the camshaft. During warm-up, it is kept within the engine cooling passages by the action of a thermostat valve which blocks off the inlet to the radiator. This valve opens at around 80° C, allowing the pump to feed water to the radiator header tank. It passes through the radiator tubes, giving off its heat to the air, before returning to the pump through an external pipe for re-circulation. Any overflow from the radiator is fed into a separate reservoir, and is sucked back into the radiator as the motor cools

cools – was used for many years. Pump circulation brings its own problems, one of which can be overcooling. Just as air-cooled engines tend to run a little too hot, liquid-cooled engines can run a little too cold. This tendency is overcome in two ways – firstly, by sealing the system with a spring-loaded filler cap, designed to keep the pressure within the system higher than atmospheric. The effect is to raise the boiling point of the liquid beyond the normal boiling point of water, enabling it to run hotter without turning the contents of the jackets into steam. The other is to have a heat-controlled valve – a thermostat – which restricts the circulation of the coolant to the jackets and thermostat housing alone until working temperature is reached. Then the valve opens progressively, to allow the coolant to be pumped to the radiator.

Water-cooling systems often have auxiliary fans, whose job is to draw air through the radiator and so ensure a cooling airflow when the bike is at a standstill, or is travelling slowly. As with the forced-air cooling system, the fan takes power from the engine to drive it and is wasteful at high speeds, when it is still revolving even though no boost to the airflow is needed. The solution, here, is to drive the fan by means of an electric motor, which is itself controlled by an independent heat-sensitive switch (another thermostat) so that it comes into operation only when the temperature of the coolant rises beyond a critical point.

Lubrication system

All the ingenuity expended upon cooling the engine would be of no avail if there was no internal lubrication, since the unit would seize solid within seconds. We all know that engines need oil: getting that oil where it is wanted is subject to almost as many variations of ingenuity as is used in cooling systems.

The simplest method, of course, is petroil – simply mixing the engine oil with the petrol. This can only be used on a two-stroke engine, where the mixture is induced into the crankcase before being transferred to the cylinder. The effect of the compression in the crankcase is to condense out some of the heavier oil content of the mixture, leaving the lighter petrol droplets still mixed with the air. The internal working surfaces are thus constantly sprayed with oil, and the cylinder walls receive a still-oily mixture during each transfer period. The system is efficient and almost foolproof – if there is fuel in the tank, then the engine is being lubricated.

Unfortunately, the petroil system is relatively wasteful. Modern techniques have brought the ratio of oil to petrol down from the heavy 1 part of oil to 16 of petrol of pre-war days to half, or even a third, of that amount now. Some two-strokes have run with a ratio of only 1 in 100 mixture. Generally speaking, however, petroil-lubricated two-strokes are profligate users of oil. Since they exhaust a proportion of the oil unburned, they are also 'dirty' engines from the environmental viewpoint. Anti-pollution regulations, increasingly, are killing off two-strokes – and the petroil engine is the first casualty.

The alternative to petroil is to meter oil to the engine through a pump. The usual method is to link the mechanically-driven pump to the throttle control, so that the amount of oil supplied is proportionate to the load on the engine. Normally, the oil is injected into the inlet port, just behind the carburettor, so that it mixes as a fine spray with the mixture being induced.

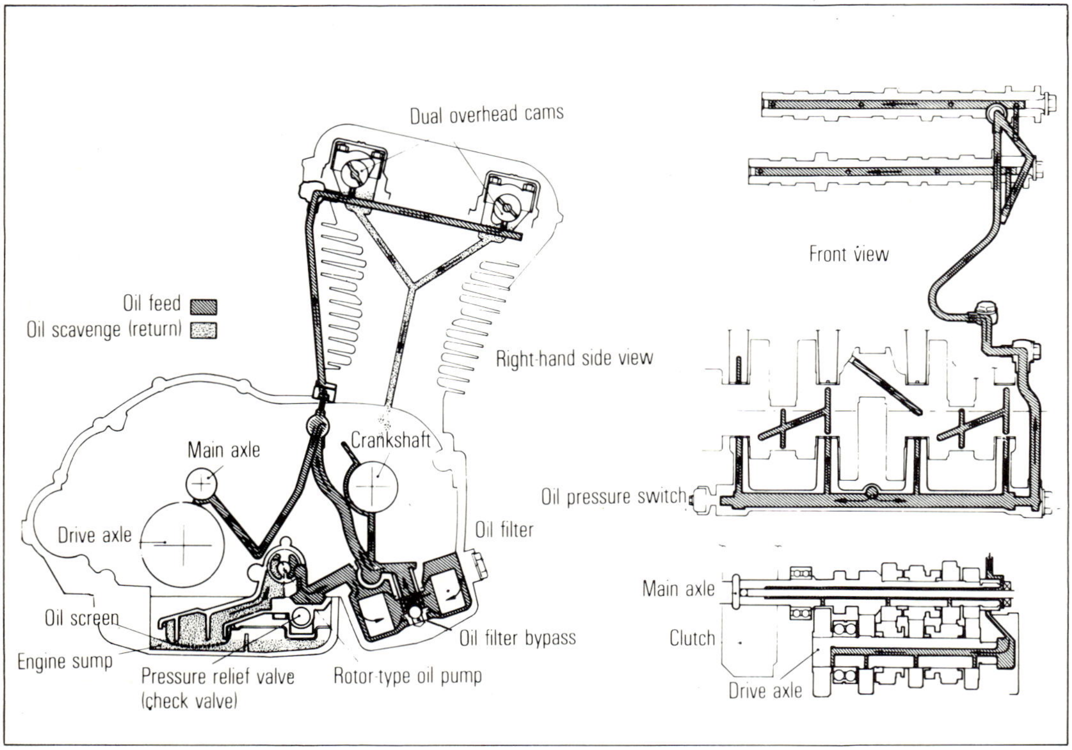

Engines depend upon oil to keep internal temperatures at workable levels. Two-strokes simply feed oil spray into the motor, and rely on splash feed in the gearbox, the pinions dipping into an oil reservoir. On four-strokes, a more complicated system is required, typified by this Yamaha XS750 circuit. The oil pump, taking its supply from the sump, delivers it through passages not just to the moving parts of the engine – at over 40 psi pressure – but also to the gearbox shafts. A by-pass valve is built into the oil filter, so that any blockage there will not cut off the supply and cause a catastrophic seizure

Four-stroke engines, in which the mixture passes straight into the cylinder, cannot use petroil lubrication. The four-stroke equivalent – splash lubrication – is rarely, if ever, used. It consisted simply of arranging the sump, containing oil, under the rotating parts, so that they would dip into it. The resulting oil spray gave liberal internal lubrication at the cost of massive oil drag, which limited the performance. Nonetheless, it was used on simple commuter four-strokes as late as the 1960s.

The more normal method is to use a wet sump – one containing oil – the level of which is clear of the major rotating components. Lubricant is drawn from this reservoir by a pump, and circulated through passages to the areas of main loading. It then returns, by gravity, to the sump. Invariably, filters are used in the system to remove impurities, since this oil constantly circulates and in doing so collects impurities and minute metallic traces which, passed back through the motor, could cause damage.

An alternative system utilises a separate oil tank, with a scavenge pump added to return the oil to the tank. This is called a 'dry sump' system.

Both wet-sump and dry-sump motors may also have an oil cooler incorporated in the circuit. This is basically a miniature radiator, which cools the oil and prevents it thinning due to heat.

Motorcycle systems operate at relatively low pressures and do not therefore normally have pressure gauges such as those fitted to cars. Instead, a warning lamp is lighted by a pressure-sensitive switch, inserted in the oil galleries, when pressure is below the safe minimum. For the same reason, excessive oil pressure does not require the heavyweight valving used on cars.

Filters are of two types – the coarse mesh strainer which prevents particles entering the pump intake; and the finer filter which removes impurities that can easily pass through the mesh. Most filters of this type are based on an element, which is discarded and renewed at regular intervals. As a safeguard, a by-pass valve is incorporated in the system so that in the event of the filter element becoming clogged, oil will still reach the engine through this valve (which will open due to pressure build up in the filter), but the oil will be unfiltered – this is preferable to having no lubrication at all.

Another widely-used filter is of the centrifugal type. This can be either a separate filter chamber bolted to the crankshaft, or a chamber formed in the clutch body. In operation, the circulating oil enters this chamber which is rotating at high speed, and the incoming lubricant is subjected to a high centrifugal force which centrifuges the impurities from the oil on to the walls of the chamber, while the cleaned oil continues circulating through the system.

Engine ventilation

We have noted how, by sealing the crankcase, a two-stroke engine can use it as a form of pump. Four-stroke engines do so too – but in this case the induced air is unproductive. The pistons in rising and falling constantly alter the crankcase pressure, and this would result in massive oil leaks if there were no means of bleeding-off the unwanted air.

This job is done by the breathing system. Before anti-pollution regulations began to take effect, the breathing system often consisted of nothing more than a pipe linked to a crude form of disc valve which enabled air to be blown straight out of the crankcase. This air usually contained a high proportion of unburned hydrocarbons, now recognised as rank pollutants.

Consequently, modern breathing systems are far more refined. Usually, a pipe leads the crankcase fumes from the engine to a filter. After passing through the filter, which in turn has a drain pipe to vent out moisture, the fumes are fed into the induction system, whence they are drawn into the combustion chambers and burned.

Bearings

Cooling and lubrication of the engine is needed to keep the bearing surfaces intact, so that the various components can move easily against each other. So, what are bearings? At one time, you could have defined a bearing as 'a member interposed between two other members so that they could move relative to each other'. Nowadays, though, improved oils and metallurgy have meant that in some instances – Honda camshafts, for example – the hard steel of the camshaft can rotate in the light alloy of a cylinder head with no need to interpose a soft-metal bearing to protect either. But, the faces that are in contact are *still* bearing surfaces. So, too, are the contact faces of the piston and the bore. You therefore have to fall back on the text-book description of a bearing as 'a locality': even if, for practical purposes, when a biker talks about bearings he is usually referring to steel races running on rollers or balls; or soft-metal plain bushes; or steel bearing shells coated with white-metal anti-friction surfaces.

Inside many four-stroke engines, there are examples of all

three types – and variations within them too. Two-stroke engines, with their considerable heat/lubrication problems, are usually designed with only ball or roller bearings, which are less demanding to lubricate than plain bearings.

A typical ball race consists of an inner track and an outer track – basically, two steel rings – held apart by a cage in which bearing balls are mounted. The cage prevents the balls bunching together and hammering against each other. Roller bearings are of similar design, but with hardened steel rollers in place of the hardened steel balls. A roller bearing will carry a greater load than an equivalent ball bearing, simply because the bearing surface – the total area of the rollers or balls transmitting the load from one track to the other – is larger than with the ball bearing.

Where a bearing has to carry a side thrust as well as a load at right angles, a tapered-roller type is often used. The normal radial loads are transmitted as before, but the axial (end) load is absorbed by the simple expedient of shaping the bearing as a truncated cone, and setting the rollers at an angle. For very heavy radial loadings – those on the small end of a two-stroke connecting rod, for example – a needle roller bearing is used. This has a multiplicity of very thin rollers, giving an enormous bearing area.

The simplest form of plain bearing is a bush, machined from soft metal or from an alloy such as phosphor bronze. Again, they are often used in small ends, where they are usually drilled for lubrication, and sometimes grooved as well. The shell-type bearing is more sophisticated. It is designed to leave a small gap between its own bearing surfaces and the journal when the engine is at rest. As the motor turns, oil is pumped into the gap, and physically separates the two components, so that the journal rides on a cushion of oil and there is no metal-to-metal contact at all. This hydrodynamic lubrication explains why shell bearings must be carefully matched to their journals. With too tight a fit, although the component will have no unwanted play, it will have no lubrication either, and the bearing surfaces will melt and seize.

Associated with bearings are the seals used to keep in the lubricant – oil, or grease. Not every bearing has a seal: typical applications are where the bearing is set in the crankcase and carries a projecting shaft. In two-strokes, the seal also has to maintain crankcase compression.

Seals are usually moulded from neoprene, or similar material, and take the form of a ring with a basically U-shaped cross-section. The main lip of the 'U' is spring loaded by the insertion of a circular coil spring, and this lip faces the oil. Any pressure brought to bear on it forces the seal into closer contact with the shaft, and so prevents leakage.

Some bearings are grease-lubricated. Usually, these are in areas of relatively low-speed rotation – wheel bearings, for example – or in near-static conditions, as with steering heads. However, grease-lubricated bearings have been used on gearboxes, and one current motorcycle (the 350 cc Jawa) has a grease-lubricated centre bearing, on its crankshaft.

Cams and valves

We have seen that the operation of a four-stroke engine is dependent upon the use of valve gear to control the induction of mixture, and the expulsion of burned gas. Unlike the two-stroke engine, the four-stroke cannot work without valves.

Although exotic valve gear has been tried many times – rotary valves; piston valves; sleeve valves – modern practice is to use the simple poppet valve. Basically, it is a metal mushroom. Its stem passes through a guide, set in the cylinder head and projecting into the port which the valve is to control. The valve head is cut to match a similarly-cut seat in the combustion chamber, and it is held on to the seat by a spring, or combination of springs, trapped between the upper face of the cylinder head and a cap fixed to the valve stem.

Driven at half the speed of the crankshaft, a cam is arranged to open the valve for predetermined periods, and to allow the spring to close it. The cam may bear directly on a bucket tappet interposed between its face and the valve stem; or it may operate the valve through a rocker – a small metal see-saw. In either case, where the cam itself is mounted above the cylinder head, the engine is known as an overhead-camshaft (ohc) type. A double-ohc engine has separate camshafts for the exhaust valves and the inlet valves, and this type almost invariably operates through bucket tappets.

The overhead-valve engine (ohv) differs from the ohc unit in having the camshaft set in the crankcase. Here, followers bear on the cam, and push up the rockers through short, circular rods called push rods. Where the camshaft is mounted high up in the crankcase, and the rods are therefore shorter than usual, the

A double overhead-camshaft arrangement – a system now gaining in popularity on superbikes. This is on the Yamaha XS750, but double ohc operation is also used by Honda, Suzuki and Kawasaki. Each cam bears directly on the tappet controlling a valve, so reducing the weight of the reciprocating parts to a minimum and extending the rev range that can be used before valve bounce sets in

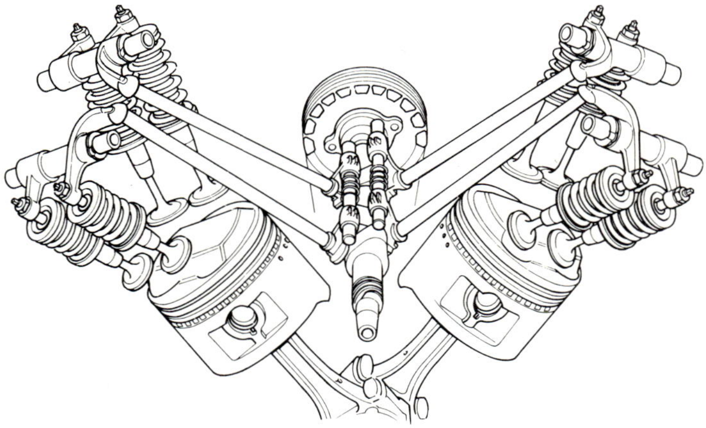

Simpler than it looks, the CX500 valve gear marks a reversion to push rod operation. The centrally-placed camshaft operates followers. These press the push rods upwards, so lifting one end of each rocker. The other end see-saws, and opens the valve. To obtain maximum breathing, this motor has four valves to each cylinder – two inlets, and two exhausts. Variations on the valve theme include twin inlets and single exhaust; and a single large inlet valve used with a smaller exhaust valve

layout is sometimes referred to as a high-camshaft layout. The most notable recent example is the Vee-twin Honda CX500, capable of revving to over 10,000 rpm, thanks to the lightness of its valve gear.

Overhead mounting of the valves permits a designer more scope in the design of the combustion chamber – one of the most critical areas. Typical chamber designs are: hemispherical; squish-type, in which the gas is arranged to swirl; pent-roof, in which high-compression ratios are possible by use of a piston with a vee-shaped crown mating with a basically inverted vee-shaped head; and the Heron type, in which the combustion chamber is formed in the piston crown, and the head surface is perfectly flat.

The number of valves to each cylinder can also be varied. It is usual to have one exhaust valve and one inlet valve, making the inlet valve the larger of the two. The object is to maximise the volume of mixture that can be induced into the cylinder during the induction stroke. Getting rid of the exhaust gases, which tend to rush out of the exhaust valve during the exhaust stroke, thanks to their inertia, is less of a problem. Even so, two valves are not always adequate. Honda – following a practice initiated by the British AJS racers of the 1950s – have equipped two of their parallel-twin engines with twin inlet valves and a single exhaust valve; and on the CX500 twin and the CBX 1047 cc 'six' have used twin inlet valves and twin exhaust valves in each cylinder.

The gain here is not merely in the capacity of the double ports to pass more mixture. Each valve is lighter, and is therefore less prone to 'bounce' on its seat at high revs. Multi-valve engines can therefore carry on producing power higher up the rev range.

A method of achieving the same result without extra valves is to adopt the desmodromic type of valve operation used on some of the Ducati vee-twins. Here, the valves are opened in the usual way by rockers, but are closed not by springs but by mechanical 'fingers' linked to the rockers. This positive closing completely eliminates valve bounce, giving the engine the ability to reach peak revs without danger of an oscillating valve ramming its head into the piston crown.

Now largely obsolete, side-valve (sv) engines have the valves mounted vertically alongside the cylinder in a valve chest. Although the valve gear is lighter compared with an ohv engine, it has a lower efficiency, since the combustion chamber has to be extended sideways into a narrow pocket above the valves, giving a poor design shape for high-speed operation. Motors of this type are sometimes called 'flat heads'.

All valve gear needs clearances if it is to work efficiently, to allow for wear and the expansion effect of heat on metal. Adjusting the tappets is one of the most familiar jobs on a bike, apart from cleaning the plugs. The most usual adjustment arrangement is to set a threaded tappet into one end of the rocker, holding it in place with a locknut. Screwing the adjuster in or out alters the clearance between the adjuster pad and the valve stem. On ohv machines, the adjuster may be arranged to operate on the push rod instead.

Bucket tappets can have adjusters operated by keys; or have the clearance between the heel of the cam (the rounded end) and the valve varied by removing a shim and replacing it with one of a different size. On side-valve engines the most usual method is to fit the adjuster to the cam follower mechanism, although on some cool-running engines adjustment is made by grinding off some metal from the end of the valve stem.

Two-stroke porting arrangements

It is not practical to use poppet or mushroom valves operated by cams in two-stroke motorcycle engines, because the relatively short duration of opening mitigates against their usefulness at very high speeds. Poppet valves have been used on some marine two-strokes for controlling entry of the mixture into the crankcase.

Referring to the two-stroke cycle explained earlier, in which the lower edge of the piston controls an inlet port and the crankcase is utilised as a pump to supply mixture to the transfer ports, this simple piston-controlled inlet porting system cannot be made really effective at *all* speeds. The reason can be briefly stated as follows: Increasing the inlet port size or prolonging the port timing, while increasing the power at high speeds, reduces both the pumping efficiency of the crankcase and the tendency to blow-back at low speeds.

To obviate this defect, two-stroke engines now commonly employ either a rotary valve or a reed valve to control induction of the mixture into the crankcase.

The rotary valve was the earliest solution to the problem. Basically, it is a disc driven by the crankshaft. On Vespa scooter engines, it is actually formed into one of the crank cheeks. As the piston closes the transfer port on its upward stroke, the rotary valve, which has previously been blocking off the inlet tract, opens. The result is a long crankcase induction stroke, and the port can be left open right up to the point at which the increase in crankcase pressure as the piston descends would normally start pushing mixture out of the motor. Some disc valves are made flexible, so that any internal pressure forces them against the inlet to improve the gas sealing. Others, like the Vespa, rely on very close machining tolerances in manufacture to give the effect of a close seal without actual contact.

Reed valves were originally developed for outboard marine engines and industrial use, but were quickly adapted to bikes. The reed is basically a thin sheet of spring steel which acts as a hinged flap in the inlet port. As the piston rises, the pressure in the crankcase drops below that of the air outside, so mixture is thrust through the inlet tract and forces open the valve. It stays open until

Tuning up modern engines calls for modern methods. The contact-breaker timing on this CB400 Honda needs to be set with the aid of a stroboscope, while to synchronise the four linked carburettors demands the use of this multiple vacuum gauge rig. Get all four needles in the same place when the engine's running, and the carburettors are perfectly tuned. It's a job that is almost impossible to do accurately by any other method, and it is common to virtually all current four-cylinder bikes

the piston, descending again, increases the pressure in the crankcase and forces the valve to close. The valve gives a double advantage – a long induction period: and no loss of mixture from the crankcase due to blow-back.

Valve timing; four-stroke engines

The timing of two-stroke engines with rotary and reed valves is largely automatic, but with four-stroke engines it is far more complicated. Designers of four-stroke engines are ever experimenting with cam forms and valve overlap in their efforts to obtain the best compromise between performance and fuel economy.

At first glance, it might be assumed, as there are four distinct strokes to each cycle of operations, the appropriate valve would open at TDC at the beginning of that stroke, and close at BDC at the end of it. In practice, this does not happen, since the column of incoming fresh gas takes time to get on the move once the valve opens. To compensate for this, the valve is therefore opened just before the piston reaches TDC – perhaps 5° of crankshaft travel in the case of a simple commuter-bike engine, or 50° with a sporty superbike – despite the fact that the exhaust valve, too, is still open at this point. This might seem to be a recipe for disaster, with the two gas streams mixing, and fresh mixture disappearing straight through the exhaust port. In fact, the depression created by the last wisps of exhaust gas rushing down the pipe is beneficial in getting the fresh gas stream on the move, and the exhaust valve is virtually closed by the time any appreciable amount of fresh charge actually enters the cylinder. That commuter bike's exhaust valve would close some 5° after TDC, and the superbike's valve 50° after TDC, giving valve overlaps of 10° and 100° respectively.

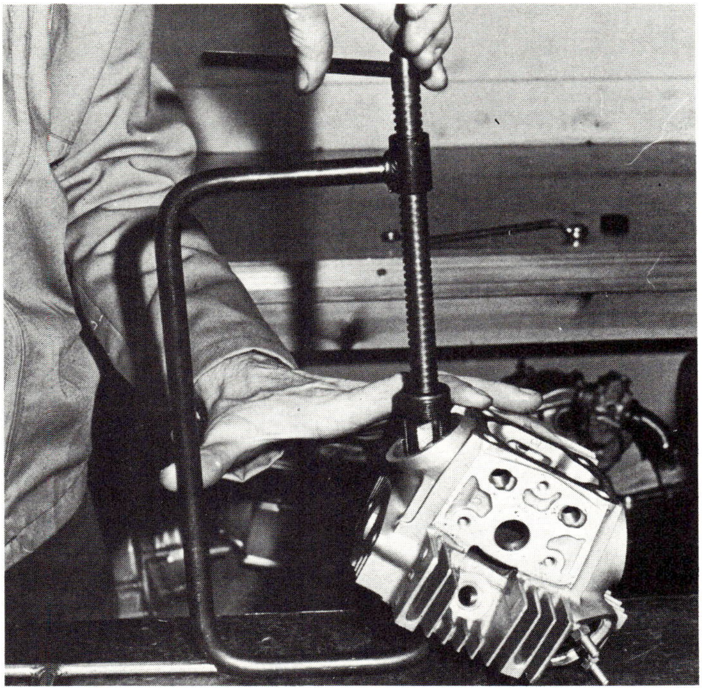

Modern oils have made decarbonising a less frequently-needed job than it was even 20 years ago, but all four-stroke valves need attention from time to time to maintain a good gas seal, since the seatings become pitted. The valves are removed with a valve spring compressor

As a general rule, increasing valve overlap to the maximum gives a steady increase in power at high engine speeds, coupled with a loss of power at low revs and a heavy fuel consumption. On racing engines, these penalties are acceptable. On road machines, they mean that the designer has to be careful to choose just the right combination for the job the bike is designed to do.

Besides overlapping the opening of inlet and exhaust valves at the end of the exhaust stroke, it is normal practice to leave the inlet valve open for some degrees after BDC at the end of the induction stroke, and to open the exhaust valve before the piston reaches BDC on the power stroke.

The late closing of the inlet valve takes advantage of the ability of the gas stream, through inertia, to overcome the initial increase in cylinder pressure as the piston starts to rise. A useful increase in the effective induction stroke can thus be gained. Taking our commuter bike and our superbike as examples again, the inlet valve would close at 20° and 65° after BDC respectively, giving an effective induction period of 205° and 295°. And, since the burning gas on the power stroke has expended most of its energy long before the piston reaches BDC, the exhaust valve is opened early – 25° before BDC on the commuter; 65° on the superbike. Burned gas is therefore already streaming out through the exhaust port even before the piston starts to rise and expel it, so giving much improved scavenging.

Scavenging Yamaha's seven-port engine

To improve the scavenging of the two-stroke engine, where the use of exhaust valves is virtually precluded, one development has been in the Yamaha seven-port engine. This utilises the non-return action of an inlet reed valve to force a small charge of fresh gas over the piston crown to help expel residual exhaust gases.

In this motor, the inlet port on the cylinder side of the reed valve is replaced by a small chamber. During induction, it acts as a normal inlet port, but controlled initially by a port cut in the side of the piston. Then, the piston skirt clears the port as well, and mixture continues to be induced in the normal way.

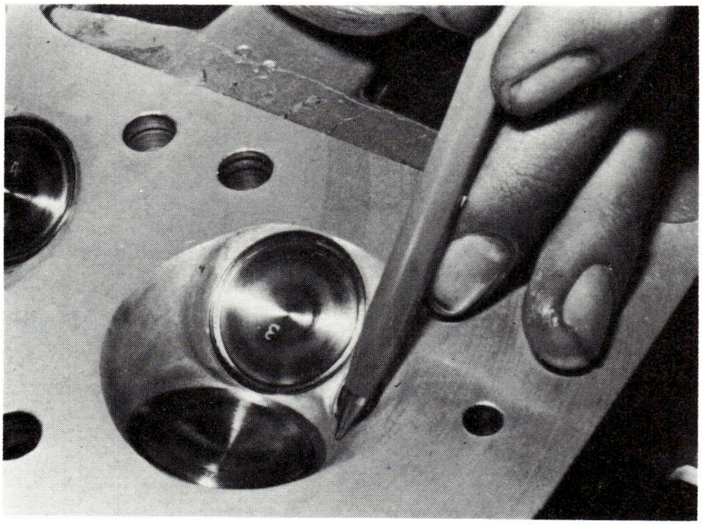

Engine tuning includes much painstaking work getting a mirror finish on the internal parts, and carefully blending out any blemishes in the combustion chambers that could lead to local overheating or to blanketing of the gas flow. All combustion chambers, too, must be equal in volume, or the engine will not run smoothly or give its full power

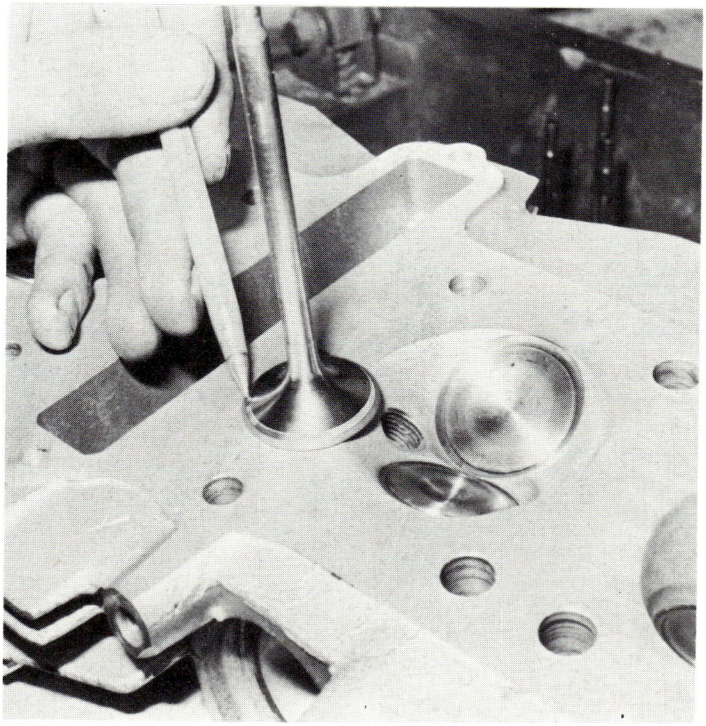

This is the ideal at which to aim – continuous line contact right round the valve head, matching it to the valve seat. Valve seat shapes are complex, however, and badly-pitted seats may need to be refaced with a cutter rather than just ground in with paste

As the piston descends, the reed valve closes. The skirt cuts off the chamber, trapping a small quantity of fresh gas. Further movement of the piston compresses the gas in the crankcase, and then opens the chamber again. The trapped mixture cannot escape, because it is now at a lower pressure than the gas already in the crankcase. Instead, it is in turn compressed, and then trapped again as the piston port seals the chamber off with further movement of the piston.

With one important difference, the rest of the operation is conventional two-stroke practice. The piston uncovers the exhaust port, and exhaust gases begin to rush out. The piston then uncovers the transfer ports, which are so sited and angled that the fresh gas streams being pumped in hit each other, and are deflected upwards into the cylinder away from the open exhaust port. But now comes the important difference. Virtually at BDC, the upper edge of the piston uncovers the small chamber containing the pre-compressed gas. The orifice formed by the piston and the walls of the chamber is so designed that this charge of gas shoots into the cylinder, across the crown of the piston, towards the exhaust port, driving any residual exhaust gas in front of it. Dilution of the freshly-induced charge higher up the cylinder is minimised, and the engine can therefore develop more power and will misfire less at light loadings.

Dismantling Yamaha XS 250 vertical-twin four-stroke engine

So how does the theory translate into practice? To illustrate the make-up of a middleweight four-stroke engine, we have chosen to show the dismantling of the Yamaha 250 motor.

Yamaha XS250 Engine Strip.
A compression test will help to determine if the engine actually needs a strip. Compression pressures are specified for every motor, together with permissible limits. Any difference between the readings of each cylinder should be within the makers' tolerance figure. Uneven compression pressures mean an imbalance of power, and the need for attention to the valves and piston rings

Work starts with draining the sump oil. A slightly warmed motor will help the oil flow more easily, and will also make the engine components more pleasant to handle. But do not allow the unit to get too hot

Below: on most current motorcycles, the exhaust systems can be detached as a unit, without breaking the pipe/silencer joint. Do this where possible, as it reduces the chance of gas or residual oil leakage at this point

It is necessary to remove the air filter housings on the Yamaha XS250. They are held by metal straps. With some other designs, it is only necessary to free the hose clamps and leave the filter in position. The tank comes off at this stage.

Below: after freeing the clamps on the inlet stubs, the carburettors are detached as a unit. Balancing the multi-carburettor layouts on modern bikes is a painstaking task, and wherever possible the instruments should be left linked so that the original settings are not lost

For engine removal – necessary on most modern bikes for major engine work – the brake pedal has to be removed, followed by the footrests. Although the rests have a fixed position, the pedal is located on splines. Lightly mark the original position, so that it can be reset without difficulty

Below: take off the kickstarter and the gear pedal. Again, both are bolted to splined shafts and it pays to mark their proper places. Then start the ancillary dismantling by removing this chain cover. Inside is the clutch cable. Slip the cable's nipple out of its trunnion, and draw the cable from its housing

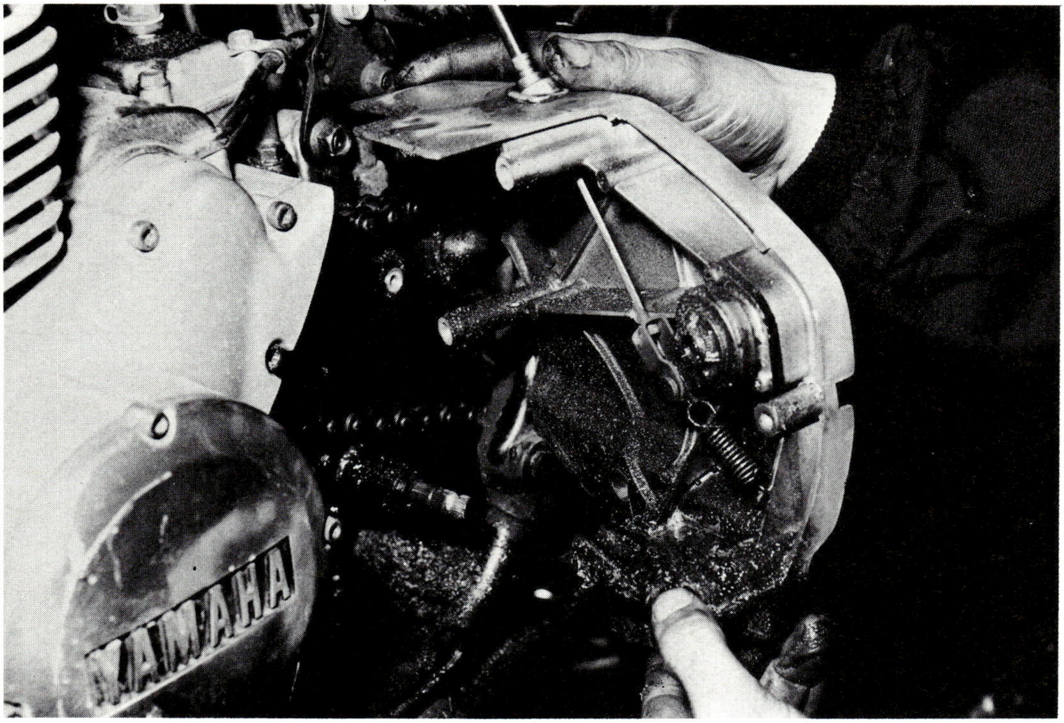

Japanese practice is to make widespread use of seals to prevent oil leakage and the entry of dust and grit. When removing seals – such as this rubber cap over the gearchange shaft abutment – always check their condition and renew on assembly if there is doubt about their serviceability

Many modern chains are endless. They have no spring link, and can only be 'broken' by use of a small chain press. The Yamaha XS250 however, uses the conventional spring link. But before removing it to break the chain, remove the nut holding the final drive sprocket. For security, the nut has a tab washer which must first be flattened. A new washer should be used when rebuilding the unit

Lubricant thrown off by the chain may conceal some of the smaller parts that need to be undone. This electrical lead on the oil warning sender is one – it is held at the terminal by a small screw

And here's another. A second small screw – invisible until the excess grease is wiped away – holds the electrical lead for the neutral indicator lamp

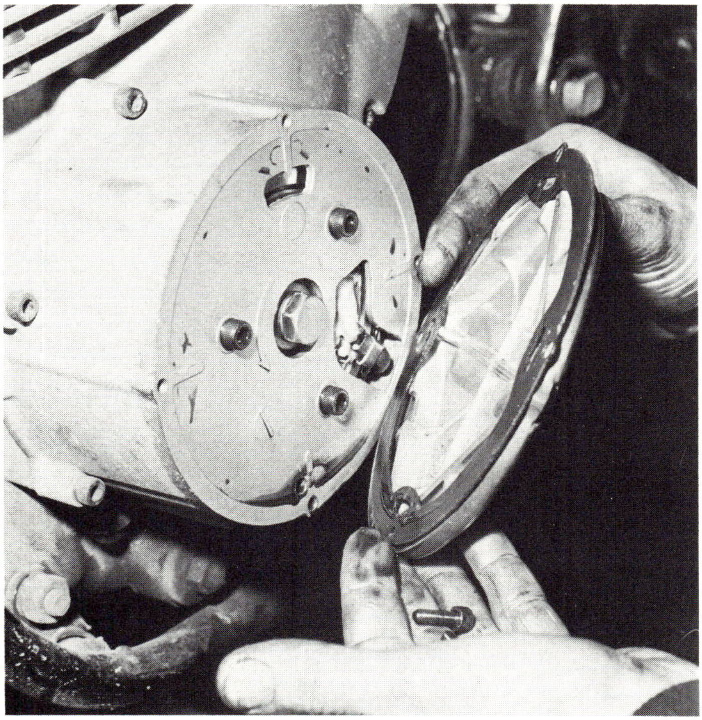

A two-part cover is used for the Yamaha's alternator. First, the outer cover is detached. It is held by four screws

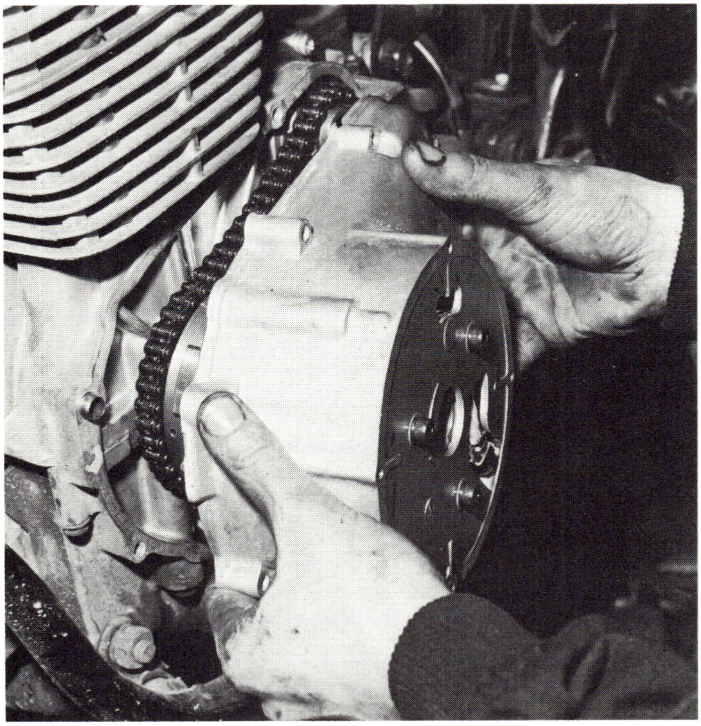

Leaving the three screws on the face of the cover untouched, the fastenings holding the inner case to the crankcase are then undone

Access to the starter motor is by removal of this plate on top of the crankcase

This chain takes the drive from the starter motor to the crankshaft, and it has a slipper-type adjuster. This must be detached before the generator rotor can be removed

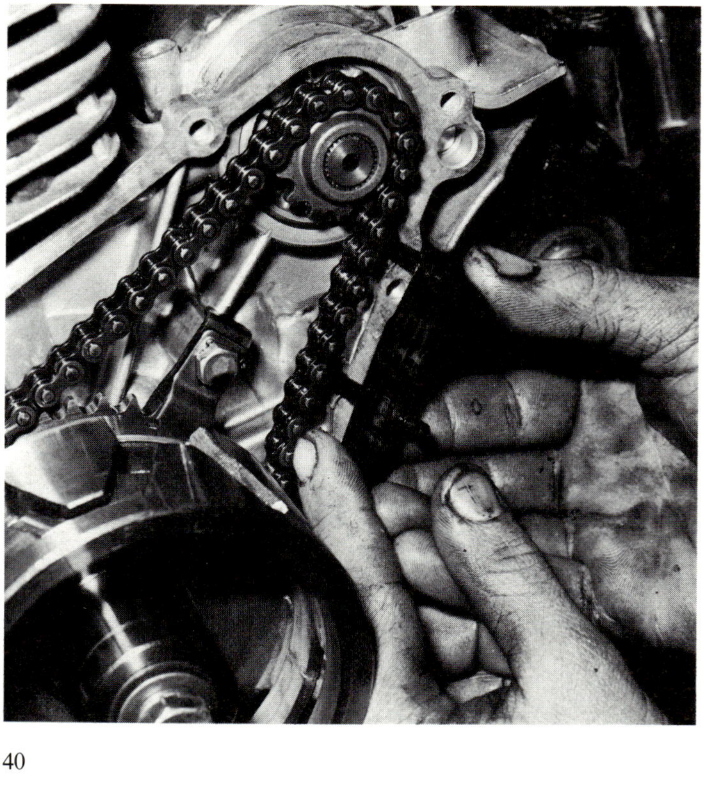

Rotor removal involves, first, undoing the securing bolt, and then inserting a puller to tug it from the shaft

Typical of current Japanese practice is the use of a security plate to locate the sprocket

This is a Woodruff key, whose job is to lock the rotor into one position on the tapered shaft. It should be pulled out with a pair of pliers. When refitting, a dab of grease will hold it in place while the rotor is offered up

How to remove the chain and sprockets. It is usual practice to pull them off together, and to refit them in the same way

When taking off the oil filter housing, always angle it upwards, as shown here. These housings usually retain a fair amount of oil, and they do not have drain plugs! The element is non-servicable and should be replaced with a new unit as a matter of course at the end of an engine strip

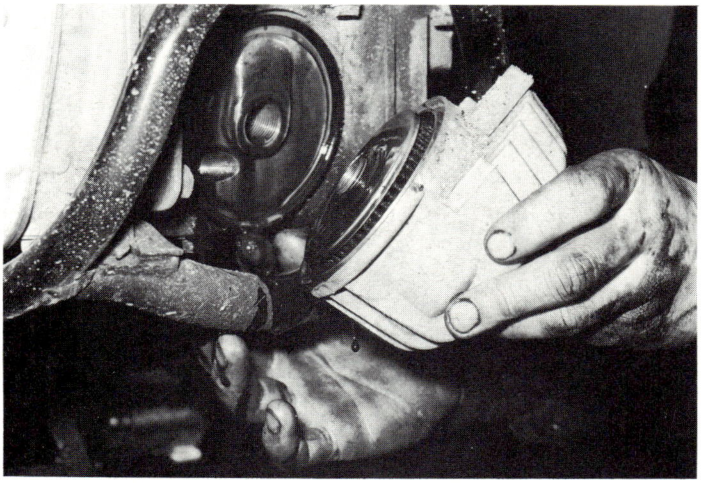

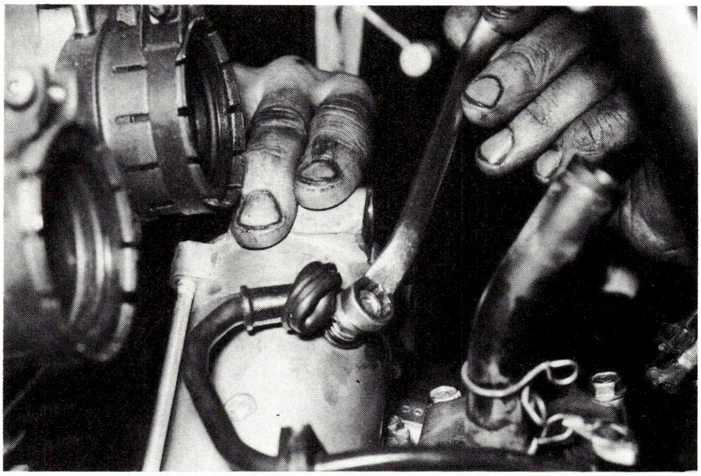

The starter motor can be removed, after undoing its holding-down bolts and main electrical lead, by pulling it from its housing. Note that its flange carries a neoprene sealing O-ring. Check its condition before refitting the motor

Turning, now, to the other side of the engine, dismantling continues with the clutch. Removal of the clutch cover reveals the clutch; the primary drive pinions; the oil pump; and the kickstarter shaft and spring

A single bolt holds the primary drive pinion to the crankshaft

Progressively unscrew the bolts that compress the clutch springs, so that the cover comes up squarely

Lift out the clutch springs, and then take off the cover plate. On this clutch, the body and the plate both carry a stamped-on arrow. On reassembly, these arrows have to be aligned

The clutch plates come away as one, and can be separated later, when they are checked for wear or damage. Those with external tangs engage into the clutch body; those with internal teeth into the clutch centre

Clutch operation is by means of a push rod, concentric with the shaft, which presses this 'mushroom' against the clutch cover plate. The 'mushroom' pulls out, and the interposed bearing ball is pushed out by pressing the other end of the rod

Some clutches are fixed to the shaft by a nut, locked by a tab washer. On the Yamaha XS250, however, a circlip is used to provide location. The washer behind it is a spacing shim, not a means of locking it

The clutch centre and clutch body pull off the shaft together. Behind the clutch is the gearchange selector mechanism

A Woodruff key locates the primary drive pinion. This pinion also drives the oil pump, and it has to be refitted with its plain face adjacent to the crankcase wall. Reverse it, and the teeth will not engage with the oil pump drive!

Another example of the use of a circlip for location – this time, on the kickstarter spindle. Here, the spacing shim is fitted outside the circlip, to give working clearance from the clutch casing

The entire kickstarter assembly pulls out. The return spring has a hook to engage on the shaped abutment of the crankcase at one end, and a tongue which slips into a slot at the lower end

When the oil pump comes away take care not to lose the locating dowel. It may remain in the crankcase, or come off with the pump

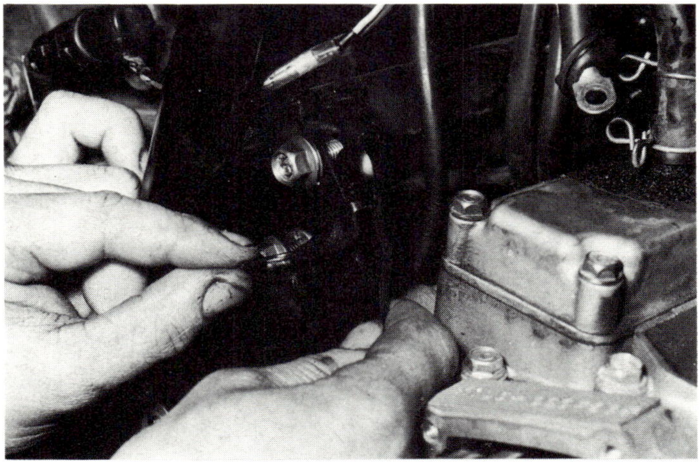

With the engine now lightened as much as possible, it must be removed from the frame for any further work to be carried out. Start by detaching the brake light switch and its bracket

Take out the two large rear mounting bolts

Next, the upper mounting has to come away. Although bushed against vibration, it is otherwise conventional. A single bolt holds the two mounting plates against the boss on the head, and a further two bolts lock the plates to the frame

Only the lower front mounting now holds the engine. With the weight supported by blocks, they are undone. The unit can now be lifted out through the right-hand frame loop. One man can do it – but it is easier if you have a friend to help

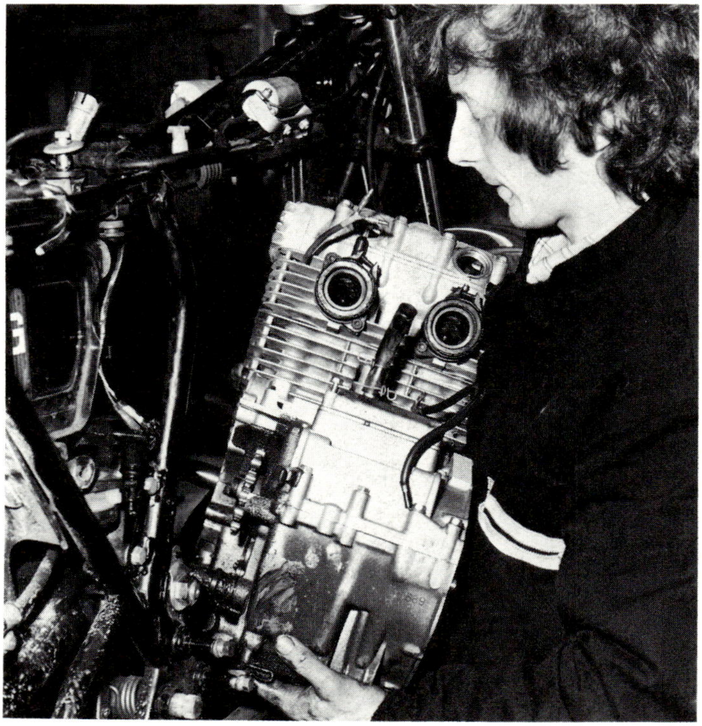

Dismantling on the bench starts with the selector mechanism. After a circlip and washer have been taken off the gear shaft on the left-hand side, the shaft is pulled out to the right. Then detach the stopper mechanism. When refitting this, the two pins must be offered up as shown, equidistant from the centre point

Lower, left: Commence stripping the top end of the engine by removing the contact breaker cover. Use a centre-punch to mark the position of the backplate relative to the head, so that the timing will not be 'lost'

Lower, right: free the centre bolt on the cam, undo the two large cross-head screws holding the back plate, and detach the breakers complete with the LT lead. Then slide the automatic advance/retard unit off the camshaft. Note the locating peg on the inner face, which engages with the slot in the boss on the auto-advance

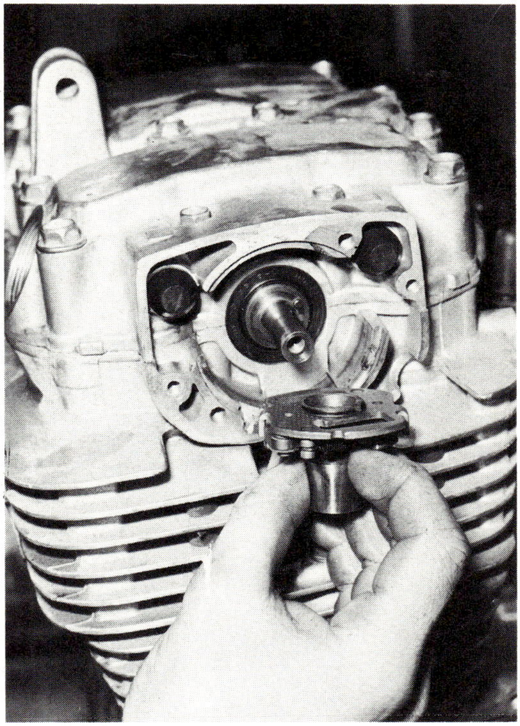

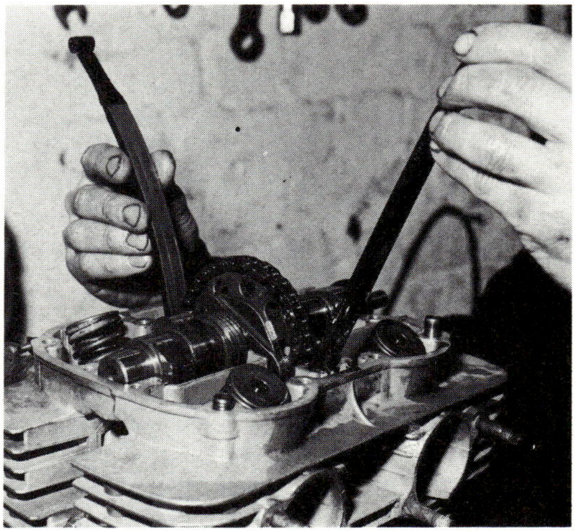

Top: the four rockers and the tachometer drive come away with the rocker box. This gives access to the camshaft-chain tensioner, behind the camwheel, which is spring loaded. Allow for this as you remove it – carefully

Top, right: the slippers are the remaining parts of the camshaft-chain tensioning mechanism. With these out of the way, the camshaft can be removed

Centre: this method is common to many Japanese ohc motors. The bolts holding the camshaft sprocket are removed, and the wheel pulled sideways. That frees the chain, which is then allowed either to slip into the camshaft-chain tunnel, or else is wired to the head

Lower: with the chain clear of the camshaft, the shaft is lifted out

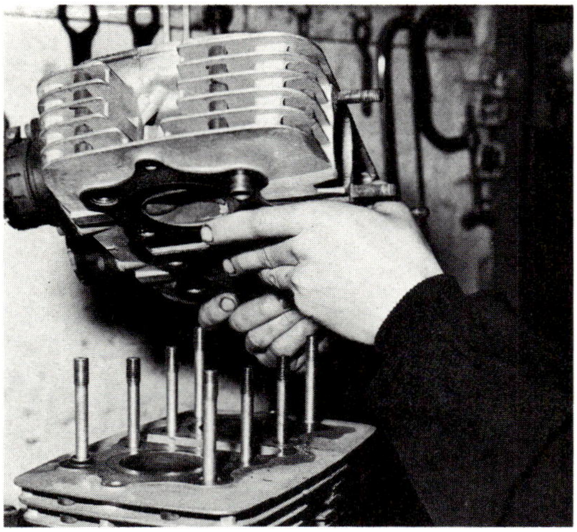

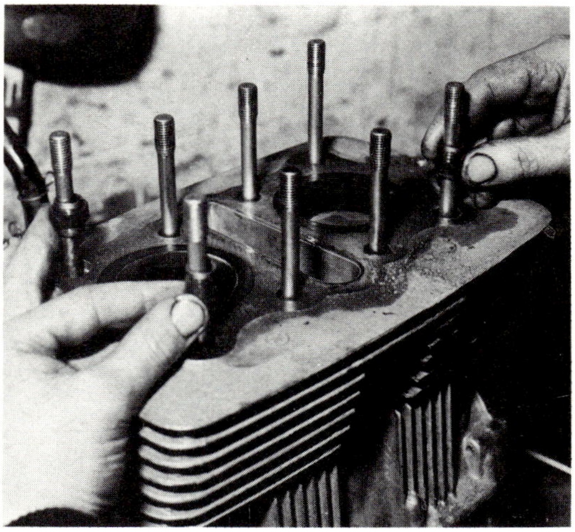

Top, left: also typical of modern practice is the eight-stud head/barrel fixing, with two auxiliary bolts by the plug holes. When freeing the head nuts, they are undone a few flats at a time, starting in the middle, and working out diagonally to each side. The idea is to release the tension evenly over the whole head, and so prevent warpage

Top, right: Japanese practice is to use the stud holes as oilways to carry lubricant to the ohc valve mechanism. Here, one stud is provided with a seal at the head/barrel joint for this purpose. Dowels are provided for accurate location, and these must always be refitted on their correct studs

Left: just as on the head/barrel joint, so with the barrel/crankcase joint. Certain studs carry locator dowels, and the rearmost also has a seal to secure the oilway

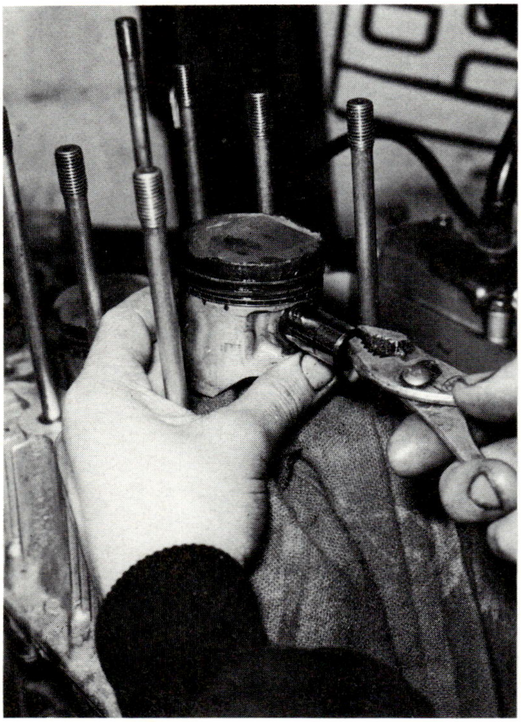

Top, left: before removing the pistons, mark each crown to ensure that they are replaced in their original positions, and facing the right way. Then remove the outer circlip and pull out the gudgeon pin. Leave the inner circlip in place

Top, right: start the bottom end strip by removing the sump base plate. Underneath is the mesh filter for the oil pick-up

Right: undo the bolts that hold the crankcase halves together; there are 21 of them. Not all are of the same length, so make a note where the longer ones go, and also note which bolts hold items such as cable clips and the earth lead

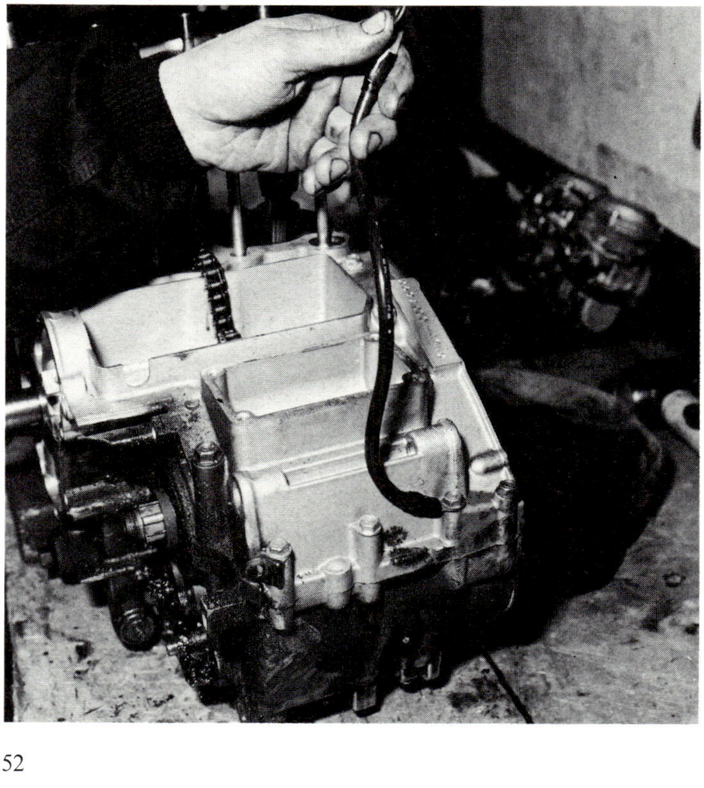

Top, left: careful jarring with a wooden block may be needed to part the crankcase. The top half comes away, leaving the internals mainly in the lower case. Remember, however, that the upper bearing shells will stay in their housings, and that they must not be lost or mixed up. Now lift out the mainshaft gear cluster first, complete with its bearings

Top, right: next comes the laygear cluster. Unless the selector mechanism is damaged, the drum and forks can stay in place. The forks are pinned to their spindles, and lifting out the clips allows the shafts to be pressed clear

Left: lastly, lift the crankshaft assembly and unbolt the big-end caps

Transmission systems

If a petrol engine was able to develop its power from tick-over speed, there would be no need for a gearbox – the power could be transmitted direct to the rear wheel. There are power units that can do this – electric motors, for example; or even steam engines.

The internal-combustion engines used on motorcycles, however, may give less than four per cent of their peak-revs power if run at only 1,000 rpm, and would be quite incapable of moving the machine away from a standstill. The solution is to interpose in the drive train a gearbox, which alters the rate at which the engine drives the rear wheel.

A typical gearbox consists of two shafts, each carrying a cluster of gears. Each pair of pinions that engage have different numbers of teeth to give a choice of, usually, four or five drive ratios. For example, if one pinion has 15 teeth and it is meshed with a 45-tooth pinion the smaller gearwheel will have to rotate three times to turn the larger gearwheel once. Between them, they produce a ratio of 15:45, which of course equals 1:3.

Using a small pinion to drive a large one is gearing down. The effect is to reduce the speed of rotation, and to multiply the turning effect – the torque. In this example, if the smaller gearwheel is driven direct by the engine at 3,000 rpm, the larger pinion will turn at only 1,000 rpm. But it will transmit three times the turning power – torque – fed into it, since it absorbs three times the number of power strokes of the engine in each revolution.

Most motorcycle transmissions work on the basis of gearing down, and there are usually three stages in which it can be employed. Firstly, there is the primary drive from the engine crankshaft to the gearbox mainshaft, which also usually carries a clutch. This stage is accomplished either through meshing pinions, or by chains and sprockets. In either case, it is usual to gear down from the crankshaft's speed of rotation by, usually, a ratio of about 1:3. Then, when the drive has passed through the gearbox, it is again transmitted to the rear wheel by chains and sprockets, or by a shaft and bevel gears, through another reduction of around 1:2 or 1:3.

At one time, the internal ratio for top gear was almost invariably 1:1 – in effect, a direct drive. Modern practice, however, is to use top gear (and sometimes the next higher intermediate gear) as an overdrive and to gear up slightly. This enables the machine to be accelerated well in the lower gears, and then to cruise at high road speeds but reduced engine speeds in the overdrive ratios. The snag is that any extra loading on the bike – a gradient; a head wind; or even a pillion passenger and luggage – will mean that a lower gear has to be used for long periods, since the engine is incapable of pulling the higher gear

Showing a typical gearbox layout, comprising two shafts, carrying meshing pinions, and a selector mechanism. The mainshaft, driven by the clutch and primary drive, passes the power to the layshaft, which carries the final drive sprocket

Lifting out the shafts from this Honda 250 engine reveals the selector mechanism – a drum whose face cams work the sliding forks to move gears into and out of engagement

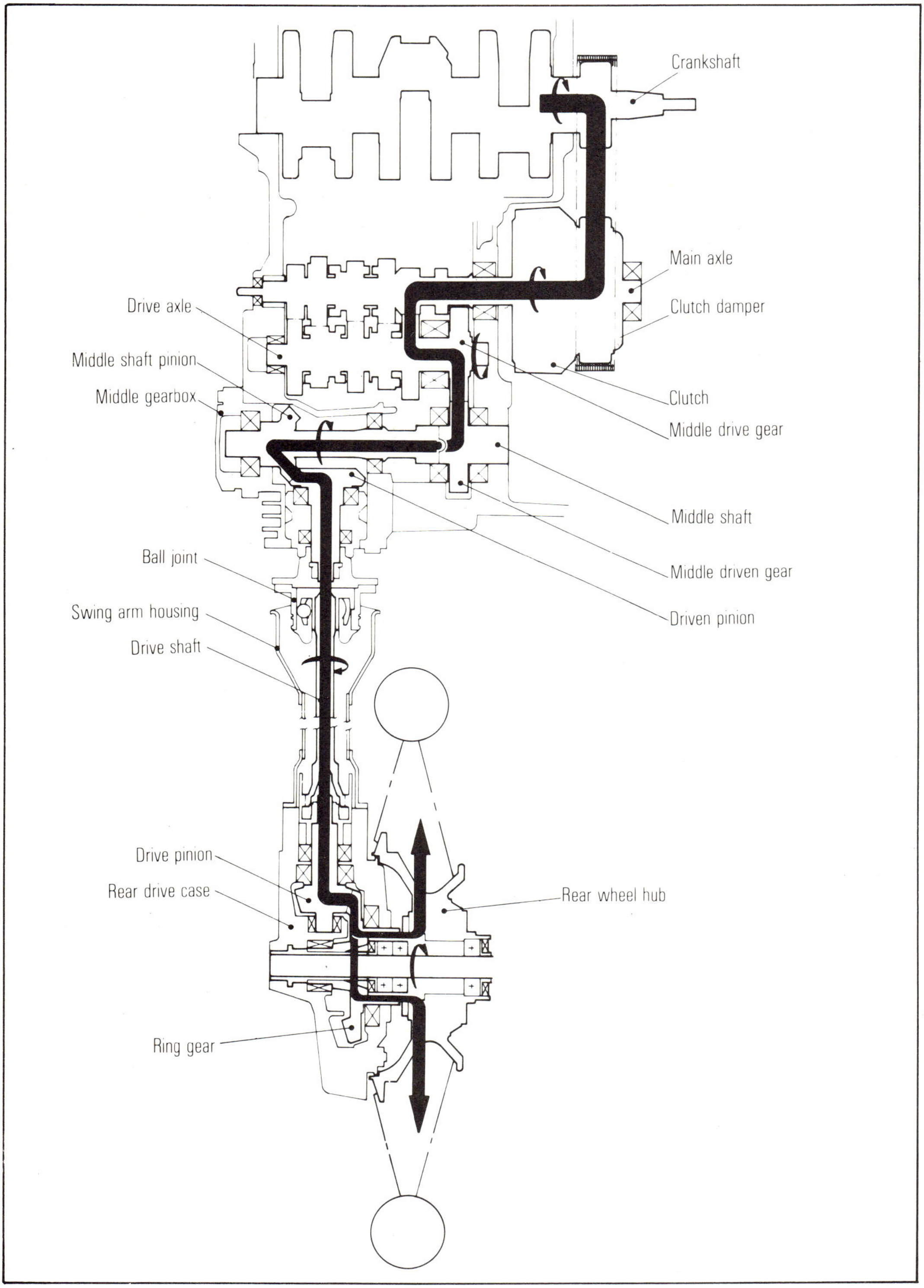

Crankshaft
Main axle
Clutch damper
Drive axle
Middle shaft pinion
Middle gearbox
Clutch
Middle drive gear
Middle shaft
Middle driven gear
Driven pinion
Ball joint
Swing arm housing
Drive shaft
Drive pinion
Rear drive case
Rear wheel hub
Ring gear

except under ideal conditions.

What is being geared-up here, incidentally, is the output shaft of the gearbox. The *overall* gear ratio remains a reduction, but by stepping up the gearing the output shaft is made to turn faster than the crankshaft. It follows, therefore, that in any given time it will receive fewer power impulses than if it were geared down, so its ability to turn the rear wheel is correspondingly reduced.

A typical 'overdrive' transmission layout is that of the Honda CB550F 'fours'. Here, the primary drive ratio is 3·246:1, and the final drive ratio is 2·00:1. The internal ratios in the gearbox are: 1st 2·353:1; 2nd, 1·636:1; 3rd, 1·269:1; 4th, 1·036:1; 5th, 0·900:1.

To obtain the overall gear ratios, all three ratios (primary; internal; secondary) must be multiplied together. The easiest way (it saves a lot of maths!) is to first multiply the primary and secondary ratios to get a single 'external' reduction. In this case, Primary × Secondary = 3·246 × 2·00 = 6·492:1. This product ratio is then multiplied by each gear ratio in turn to give the following overall ratios:

1st, 2·353 × 6·492 = 15·28:1;
2nd, 1·636 × 6·492 = 10·62:1;
3rd, 1·269 × 6·492 = 8·24:1;
4th, 1·036 × 6·492 = 6·73:1;
5th, 0·900 × 6·492 = 5·84:1.

The overall ratios show precisely how many times the engine has to turn to make the rear wheel revolve once – which also tells us how many power strokes are applied to each revolution of the wheel. In bottom gear, for example, this four-cylinder engine turns 15·28 times to one turn of the back wheel, and since a four-cylinder engine fires twice in each revolution, that means that the power of nearly 31 strokes is being brought to bear in that distance.

In top gear, the engine turns 5·84 times for the same distance covered by one turn of the back wheel, so the power applied is only that of 11 power strokes. That is why the bike will climb a steep hill in bottom gear, when use of top gear would simply 'stall' it.

There is also one further factor to consider when dealing with gearing – the diameter of the rear wheel. If a rear wheel has a rolling diameter of 24 in, it will travel a distance of just over 75 in (circumference of wheel = πd) in one revolution. Apply the same power through the same gearing to a wheel with a rolling diameter of 18 in, and the power is applied over a distance of only 55 in. The smaller diameter wheel is therefore equivalent to a lower gearing, even though mechanically everything else remains the same. Conversely, using a larger-diameter wheel raises the gearing.

Inside the box

All current motorcycle gearboxes work on the constant-mesh system, in which each gear on the mainshaft is engaged with a gear on the layshaft, and selection is made by locking the appropriate pair of gears together. A typical example of this type of gearbox is the unit fitted to the Suzuki GT500, shown on page 58.

Power is fed in to the mainshaft and since all five pinions are solidly fixed to the shaft it is transmitted to all five meshing pinions on the layshaft. With the gears in neutral (1), however, none of the layshaft pinions are locked to the shaft, and all five simply freewheel. No power is therefore transmitted.

When the gear pedal is operated to select first gear (2) a sliding hub, fixed by spines, moves along the layshaft. This hub has pegs (drive dogs) machined on its side faces. Similar dogs are machined

Opposite: the power flow through a current superbike – the shaft-driven Yamaha XS750. In this design, the drive is turned through a right angle to enable a shaft to be used with the transverse-crankshaft engine

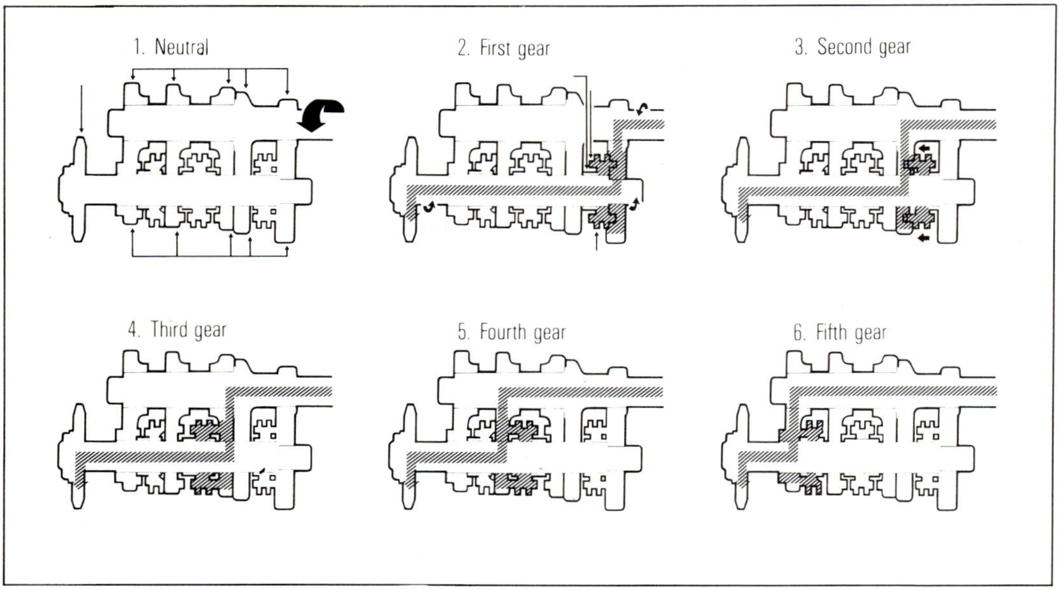

Illustrating power flow in a 5-speed gearbox according to gear selector position.

on the side faces of the pinions, or matching holes may be formed in the pinion itself. The dogs engage, and the previously free-wheeling gear is locked to the shaft. Power is now transmitted through the pair of pinions, through the selector hub, through the splined layshaft, to the final drive sprocket. While the first-gear pinion is locked to the layshaft, the remaining gears continue to free-wheel on it.

When the gear pedal is moved to select second gear (3) the hub moves out of engagement with the first gear pinion and, sliding in the opposite direction, engages its other set of dogs with the second-gear pinion. That in turn is locked to the shaft, and the power is then transmitted through it. To select third gear (4) and fourth gear (5) a second sliding hub is brought into action. As it moves to engage the third-gear pinion, the first slider is pulled out of engagement with the second-gear pinion and returns to its neutral position. The final movement of the pedal to engage fifth gear returns the third/fourth gear sliding hub to its neutral position, and moves a third sliding hub to lock the fifth-gear pinion to the shaft (6).

The mechanism that moves the sliding hubs consists of three selector forks, each of which has a pair of prongs to engage in continuous grooves cut in the sliding hubs. These forks are free to slide on a shaft and are themselves moved sideways by a selector drum mounted alongside it. The drum has a series of cam grooves cut in it, in which hardened steel pins engage – one pin to each fork. Moving the gear lever rotates the drum, and the pins – following the cam grooves – move the selector forks sideways to provide the gear selection pattern.

Only a few current machines now have separate gearboxes – usually, these are bikes such as the BMW or Moto Guzzi, where the engines are mounted across the frame – and stripping a gearbox entails removing the engine from the frame and dismantling it to the point at which the crankcases can be split and access to the gears obtained. The operations

The selector arm is double-acting, so that it can turn the selector drum either way, depending on whether the gear pedal is lifted or depressed

To ensure accurate engagement, the end of the selector drum carries a star cam, on whieh a spring-loaded stopper arm bears

involved are shown in the strip sequence in Chapter Two. However, if the problem is in the gearchange selector mechanism it can often be tackled with the unit in the frame, since it is almost general practice to have the selector mechanism within the primary drive casing, accessible once the oil has been drained and the cover (and perhaps the clutch) has been removed.

With the selector mechanism bared, replacing the gear pedal will allow it to be operated and its action checked. The visible part of the selector drum has a plate carrying rollers, on which the gear-selector ratchet bears. Light springs maintain contact between the upper and lower selector ratchet teeth. The drum can rotate in either direction.

The positive location mechanism which rests against the selector-drum rollers is also spring-loaded and weakening, stretching or actual breakage of any of the springs will cause poor or difficult gear selection.

Damage to the gear selector mechanism is usually caused by violent or over-hard use of the gear lever by a ham-footed rider. Gearboxes are designed to operate smoothly and without too much effort. If undue force is required to change gear, then there is definitely something wrong with the gearbox (or clutch) which should be investigated.

Camplate gear selector. – A camplate gear selector mechanism is the alternative to the drum gear selector. Japanese bikes usually have drums, but both Norton and Triumph – as well as the majority of now-defunct British manufacturers – used the camplate method of controlling the action of the gear selector forks within the gearbox casing.

The camplate rotates on a central spindle within the gearbox, while the selector forks follow grooves or slots cut into the face of the camplate. It is this movement of the selector forks following the camplate grooves that selects the gear required by the rider.

Wear can (and does) occur on the selector-fork pins that slot into the camplate, on the camplate grooves, and on the selector forks themselves. All create a sloppy movement in the gear selection train and imprecise engagement of the pinions, resulting in false neutrals or gears that jump out of engagement.

Inspection of the selector forks and pins, as well as the camplate grooves, will usually reveal any excessive wear. The only solution to the problem is renewal of all worn components.

Another item which sometimes (but rarely) causes gear selection problems is the camplate plunger. The plunger is spring-loaded and presses firmly against the outer edge of the camplate in which slots or notches are machined. As the camplate rotates to change gear, so the camplate plunger slides around the outer edge of the plate to locate in the notches and ensure that the gear selection operation is positive.

Wear on the outer edge of the camplate, when the plunger location notches become smooth edged, or on the plunger head which may lose its sharpness, will allow over-selection of the gears. In other words, the camplate will turn beyond its correct position for perfect pinion engagement, once again causing the pinions to jump out of gear or find a false neutral.

The camplate plunger is normally located in the gearbox casing and may be removed without dismantling the gearbox, simply by unscrewing the large retaining nut on the base of the gearbox (*not* the oil drain plug!) and lifting out the plunger and its spring.

The slightest piece of swarf, or a weakened plunger spring, can cause the camplate plunger to malfunction. It is easy to check the operation of the plunger simply by compressing it in its housing bolt. The movement should be smooth, with no signs of sticking or binding. Before refitting, clean the plunger, its spring, and the housing bolt, lubricate with gear oil, and reassemble.

Positive stop mechanism. – The positive stop built into the gear selector mechanism allows the gearchange to be made by the rider's foot, leaving both hands free to operate the handlebar controls.

The principle of operation of the positive stop is fairly simple. It operates on a pawl and ratchet system to rotate the camplate selector or gear selector drum in a clockwise or anti-clockwise direction.

On British motorcycles, the gearbox has an inner and outer cover, both of which carry vital components in the gearchange train. The outer cover contains the gearchange pedal and shaft (as well as the kickstart shaft) and on the inside of the cover is the gear selector pawl mechanism.

These selector pawls engage with the gear selector quadrant, which is mounted and pivots in the inner cover and is likewise engaged on the gearbox camplate. The gear selector pawls are spring-loaded, to maintain contact with the ratchet on the selector quadrant. However, they are also chamfered so that they only operate in one direction. So, if the gear lever is pushed downwards, only one of the pawls engages in the quadrant ratchet, causing it to move. In fact, the second pawl does not engage in the ratchet until the gear lever is purposely moved upwards beyond its centralised position, which is automatically maintained by a two-way return spring.

As the gear lever returns to its central position, the selector pawl engaged in the ratchet rides on its chamfer, out of its original location, to align with the next notch on the quadrant. A further depression of the gear lever will cause yet another movement of the quadrant and rotation of the camplate.

The two selector pawls ensure movement of the quadrant in both directions; so gearchanges may be made from first to sixth gear, or in the reverse order, with the gear lever returning to the centralised position after each selection.

Obviously, there are a number of faults that can occur with the positive stop gearchange mechanism, but fortunately, they are all normally easily cured without resort to major engine stripdown work.

One of the most common is a broken gear lever return spring. The symptom of this fault is a gear lever which, when operated will select a gear, but then fail to return to the central position. The lever may be centralised by foot and the next gear selected, but it is a laborious task and obviously something which should be remedied as soon as possible.

Normally, this simply entails removing the outer cover or primary drive cover to expose the positive stop gearchange mechanism. A broken gear lever or gearshaft return spring will be immediately apparent and the cure is a simple renewal job.

Another common failure is where a pawl fails to engage on the quadrant ratchet or on the selector drum rollers. Once again, it is a matter of removing the outer cover or primary drive casing and inspecting either the selector pawls or the selector drum operating mechanism.

Sometimes the selector pawls stick in their housings, due to a little swarf or grit; or the selector drum operating mechanism suffers a spring failure. Careful cleaning and lubrication of the pawls or renewal of the broken spring is straightforward and normally cures the fault. However, excessive wear on the quadrant ratchet face or on the pawls will sometimes cause bad engagement or slipping. In either instance, the cure is renewal of all worn components.

The clutch

Just as vital as the gearbox, the clutch provides the means of moving the machine away from a standstill, changing gear, and re-engaging neutral. It does it by temporarily disconnecting the drive from the engine to the gearbox, and allowing it to be taken up again gradually and smoothly.

The clutch is basically a simple device. It consists of a body and

All bikes have friction drive! Only the pressure exerted by these springs on the plates in the clutch allows the power to be transmitted from the engine to the gearbox

The free-running clutch body is driven by the crankshaft, and its centre is keyed to the gearbox mainshaft

a clutch centre; plain plates and friction plates; springs to hold them together; a pressure plate; and an operating mechanism.

It is usual, nowadays, for the clutch body to be driven by gear from the crankshaft. The clutch centre is bolted to the gearbox mainshaft, and there is no mechanical connection between the two. With the plates and springs removed, the clutch body could be turned freely – it rides on a bearing – and so could the clutch centre.

To transmit the engine's power, friction is used – the friction between the lined and plain plates of the clutch. The plates differ not just in being, alternately, lined and plain. They also differ in their fixings. Half of them – usually the lined friction plates – are made with tongues on their outer periphery, and these tongues engage in slots cut in the clutch body. Some designs use toothed plates engaging in splines, but the principle is the same. All these plates have plain central apertures, so that they can sit over the clutch centre, but are not connected to it.

The plain plates, however, have tongues or teeth formed round the central aperture to engage with slots or splines on the clutch centre. Their outer periphery is smooth, so that they have no connection with the clutch body.

Turn the clutch body and all the friction plates will move with it, and all the plain plates will remain still. Turn the clutch centre, and all the plain plates will move and the friction plates will remain still.

It is the pressure plate and springs that complete the package. The plate is loaded by the springs against the inner 'core' of alternating plain and friction plates, pressing them together so hard that they revolve as one solid mass. Now, as the clutch body

The drive is passed from the body to the clutch driven plates through the tangs, which engage in the slots in the body. The interposed friction plates are splined to the clutch centre

Chain care starts with lubrication. Regular spraying with a special chain lubricant helps, since the rollers – even on the latest 'sealed' chains – should never be allowed to run dry. But sprayed-on lubricant will not enter all the chain's bearing surfaces

The answer is to remove the chain, clean it, and then immerse it in a bath of molten chain grease. This ensures that the lubricant enters every crevice. After treatment, the chain is drained and allowed to dry before refitting

rotates, it turns the friction plates, which turn the plain plates, which turn the clutch centre, which transmits the drive to the gearbox. To free the drive, a rod or a cam – operated by a cable linkage from the handlebar lever – presses the pressure plate away from the driven plates. Relieved of the spring pressure that was holding them together, the plates continue to turn, but with insufficient friction between them to transmit the drive. Slowly releasing the lever progressively re-applies the spring pressure, and the drive takes up smoothly as the plates skid over each other, until the drive is again 'solid'.

Chain final drive

When properly lubricated and tensioned, the roller chain is one of the most effective methods of transferring power from the engine/gearbox to the rear wheel. The pity is that in far too many instances the final drive chain is totally neglected and this not only causes rapid wear of the chain and the sprockets on which it runs, but also creates a heavy power loss.

In extreme cases, it has been known for a badly worn chain to ride up the gearbox sprocket, break and jam into the gearbox casing, smashing the crankcases. The big Honda CB750 was prone to this failing which was brought about by rider neglect.

Chain care is one of the vital weekly maintenance tasks on any motorcycle so equipped. It takes only seconds to assess whether a rear chain needs adjusting or lubricating, and the actual task takes little more than five minutes on the majority of modern machines.

Some manufacturers recommend that the chain only be inspected and lubricated every 1,500 miles. Ignore this advice and apply commonsense to the job. Let's face it, if the bike has just completed a 200-mile run in pouring rain, there's unlikely to be any lubricant left on the outer rollers of the chain or the sprockets. If the chain looks dry then it needs lubricating; it's as simple as that.

To decide whether a chain requires adjusting, it is necessary to place the motorcycle on its centre stand and rotate the rear wheel while at the same time checking the up-and-down play on the lower run of the chain. Find the chain's tightest spot and check that it does not have any more than ¾-in total movement. If it has, then it will need adjusting.

The majority of motorcycle rear wheels are retained by a through spindle which has a castellated nut with split pin at one end and a plain end drilled to take a tommy bar at the other. By removing the split pin and loosening the retaining nut, the chain can be adjusted using the pair of adjuster bolts, one on either side of the rear fork legs.

The adjusters have wheel alignment notches cut into their upper surface which have to correspond equally on both sides with the alignment marks on the fork legs.

To adjust the chain, it is simply a matter of undoing the locknuts on the two adjusters and then tightening the bolts equal amounts to draw the rear wheel backwards to tension the chain. When there is a maximum of ¾-in up and down movement on the lower chain run at its tightest point, it is correctly adjusted.

Finally, check that the wheel alignment marks are equal, tighten the wheel spindle and re-insert the split pin, then tighten the locknuts on the chain adjusters.

It is common practice among manufacturers to fit chains without a split link, but with a 'soft' link paint-marked for recognition when the chain has to be split for

Here is a worn chain. Held like this, the minute extra clearances caused by wear between the pins and the bushes are shown by the chain bowing under this test. Maximum permissible bow in a drive chain is 130/150 mm

And here's what the worn chain did to the rear wheel sprocket. Every tooth has been distorted into a hooked shape, and the entire secondary drive is fit only for scrap

Many bikes do not have split links to enable the chain to be removed. Instead, there is a special joining link, usually made obvious by being painted, or else finished in a light-metal colour

With the split link chain, use pliers to ease the spring circlip off the pins, and then slip off the side plate. Always ensure that the closed end of the spring circlip faces the direction of chain rotation. This is an obvious safety measure

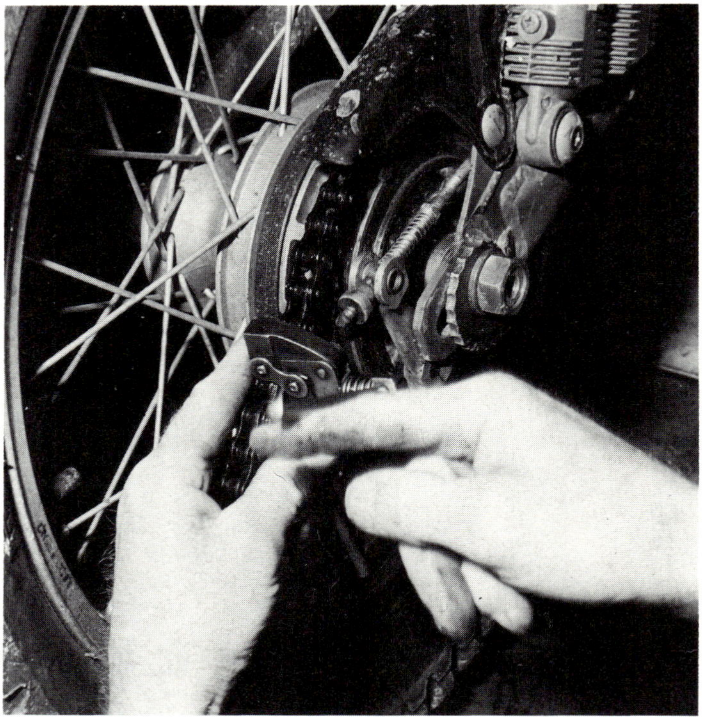

One-piece chains are removed by punching out the joining link, using a chain breaker. When this is done, a conventional spring link must be fitted on assembly – it is satisfactory for power outputs up to 60 bhp. Otherwise, it is a professional job to rivet-in a new link

replacement by the dealer. To remove the chain for boiling in chain grease – probably the most effective way of obtaining effective lubrication inside the rollers – it is necessary to have a chain link breaker.

One way of greatly extending rear chain life is to have a swap chain made up identical in size and length to the one fitted. This swap chain is cleaned and greased ready for fitting and when the chain on the bike looks worn and dry, simply pull on the swap chain by hooking on to the split link of the chain being removed.

The dry chain can then be thoroughly cleaned in a paraffin bath and hung up to dry. Then it can be immersed in a molten grease to penetrate inside the rollers. This cleaned and lubricated chain then becomes your next swap chain. This process can be carried out every 1,000 miles in a matter of half-an-hour and save pounds in having to buy replacement chains. While the chain is on the bike, it can be sprayed with one of the proprietary chain lubricants.

The latest development in roller chains for the larger capacity 'superbikes' is the sealed roller chain. Each individual roller has lubricant sealed in by small neoprene O-rings at either side. The chains are incredibly expensive, but do last. However, constant high speed with a chain that has no lubricant on the outside of the rollers or on the sprockets could soon break down the seals, so even though your superbike may have a 'superchain' fitted, it is still vitally important to lubricate the outside of the rollers and the sprockets.

Shaft final drive

The alternative to chain drive to the rear wheel is shaft drive, and

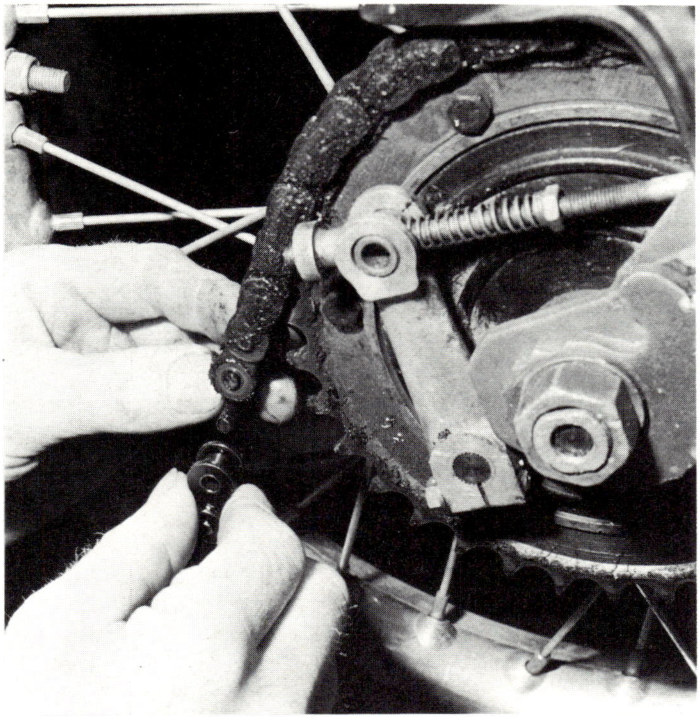

The easy way to renew a chain is to use the old one as a 'pull-through'. Hook the new chain on to old one, using the split link

Now tug the other end of the old chain to draw the new one into position

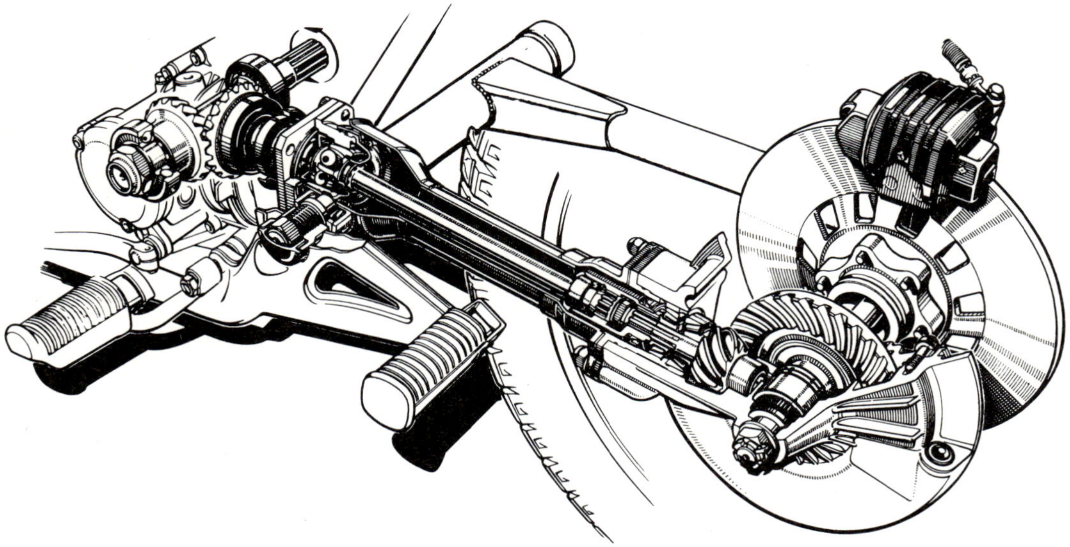

The countershaft (layshaft) on the XS750 powers the drive shaft through an outboard-mounted bevel gear. To transmit the drive at all angles of the shaft, the XS750 uses a constant-velocity joint, which is similar to those employed to give absolutely smooth transmission in front-wheel drive cars

recently more manufacturers have taken up the option to provide motorcyclists with a virtual maintenance-free final drive system. Honda, Yamaha, Moto Guzzi, and MV Agusta have all followed in the footsteps of BMW, who produced their first shaft-driven motorcycle as long ago as 1923.

A shaft drive is basically simple, but it needs to be equipped with a universal joint to accommodate the movement of the rear suspension, and since its joint cannot be absolutely concentric with the pivot point of the rear suspension – with which it must move – the shaft also needs to be equipped with a splined sliding joint to allow it to telescope as the suspension rises on bump.

The shaft transmits its drive through a pair of bevelled gears, mounted in a light-alloy housing, and these feed the power through splines or pegs to the rear wheel hub. The gears employed nowadays are not straight-cut bevels – these are unacceptably noisy in operation – but have curved 'hypoid' teeth, giving quieter operation at the expense of greatly increased pressures between the engaging teeth. For that reason, these drives have to be lubricated by an EP (extreme pressure) gear oil (also known as a hypoid oil).

In practice, shaft drives are trouble-free and virtually maintenance-free as well. Their mechanical efficiency is lower than that obtainable with chain drive, but bike engines now have power to spare, and the loss involved can be accepted.

As with the gearbox, shaft drive requires the correct grade and amount of oil to be changed or topped up at recommended intervals. Providing this simple maintenance task is carried out regularly, there is little else that can be done without specialised tools to work on the precision-built shaft drive assembly.

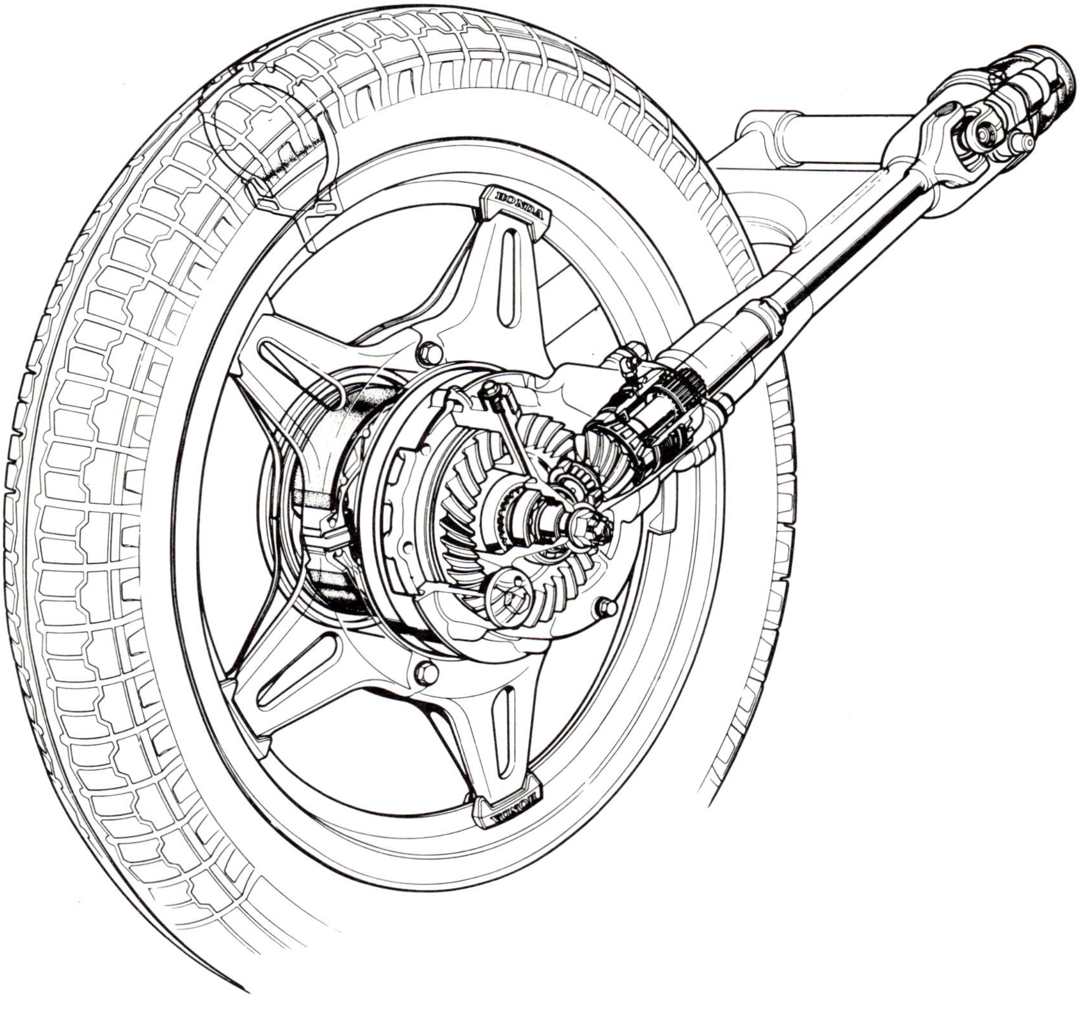

By contrast, the Honda CX500 drive shaft is operated direct from the gearbox, and is able to use a simpler double-universal coupling

Transmission shock absorbers

Some form of shock-absorbing mechanism is built into most transmission systems, to smooth out the pulsations of the engine. With shaft-drive machines, it is usually incorporated in the transmission mechanism itself, taking the form of a pair of face cams held tightly together by a heavy-duty spring, but free to move radially, relative to each other, within the controlled limits permitted by the spring.

With chain final drives, it is more usual to literally 'cushion' the drive by transmitting it through a series of vanes interspersed with rubber blocks, so arranged in the rear sprocket that the drive to the wheel passes through the rubber. blocks. This is referred to as a cush-drive rear hub.

Carburation

It's called a petrol engine: but in fact the motor in your bike runs mainly on air. The device that allows it to do so is the carburettor, which takes petrol from the tank and air from outside, and turns them into a combustible mixture by atomisation.

In general terms, this mixture has to average out at 14 parts of air to one of petrol – which may not sound a particularly difficult proposition. Nor would it be, save for one slight snag. That is the ratio *by weight*: but an engine operates *by volume*. Since petrol is considerably heavier than air, the problem facing the carburettor designer then becomes one of delivering, reliably, just one cubic centimetre of petrol to every 10,000 cc of air. So, a bike with an engine capacity of 100 cc has to draw in, each time the cylinder is charged, 99·99 cc of air mixed with just one hundredth of a cc of petrol.

This problem is made more difficult by the engine requiring this volume of mixture only under full throttle conditions. At intermediate speeds, when less than a full charge is being induced, the amount of air taken in has to be reduced, and the already microscopic amount of petrol has to be cut even further.

Years of careful development have resulted in the production of carburettors that can produce exactly the right mixture for each engine requirement, and go on doing so reliably for tens of thousands of miles under all conditions. And the resulting instruments are remarkably uncomplicated as well – virtual masterpieces of unobtrusive production engineering.

The basic parts of the carburettor comprise a reservoir of petrol (float chamber); a venturi (choke) through which the air is drawn; jets of differing sizes to meter the petrol; a throttle valve, to control the air flow; and a second control to temporarily increase the amount of fuel and provide a petrol-rich mixture for cold starts. Misleadingly, this device is also called a 'choke' (in the US, it is known as a 'strangler') since it operates by blocking off part of the air intake. An alternative to the choke is a rich-mixture control, which opens up an auxiliary feed to add extra petrol to an unaltered flow of air.

The float chamber is the heart of the operation. In design, it is much like the familiar domestic cistern. It has a float, which rises with the petrol, and the float operates a tapered needle set in the fuel inlet. When the chamber is full, the needle is hard home in its housing (the needle valve) and the flow of petrol from the tank is cut off. As the fuel in the float chamber is used up, the level falls and the float sinks with it. This releases pressure on the needle, which moves away from its seat and allows more fuel to enter. When the level is again correct – and float chamber fuel levels are

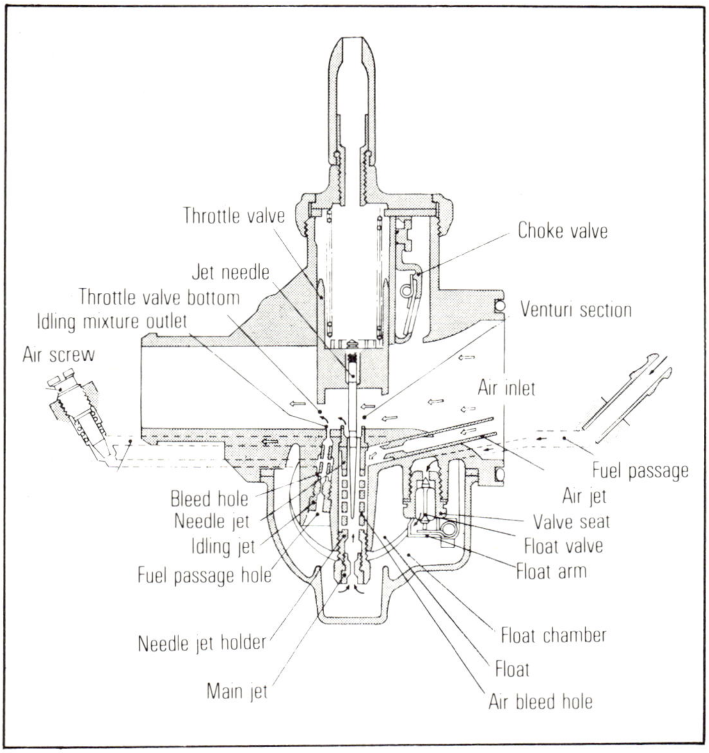

Most bikes still use this simplest form of carburettor, in which a needle jet and a cutaway slide provide the balance of the mixture, aided by a slow-running jet for low-speed operation. This illustration of a Keihin carburettor is reproduced by courtesy of Honda

critical to around plus or minus half a millimetre – the supply is again cut off. The practical result is to maintain a constant level in the float chamber just as long as there is fuel in the tank.

Modern practice is to immerse the jets in the float chamber. Older carburettors had a separate chamber, with the bottom linked to a jet well in the base of the carburettor. Each jet is a finely-drilled brass screw, the size of the drilling being such that the jet will pass a certain maximum flow of petrol, but no more. Each jet has an outlet in the carburettor venturi.

The main jet differs from the other jets in being mounted within a second metering device called the 'needle jet' or 'emulsion tube'. This is a relatively large-diameter tube with accurately-finished sides, into which projects a tapered needle controlled by the throttle. When the throttle is closed the needle is low down in the jet, cutting off all but a tiny ring of the jet from the venturi. Opening the throttle lifts the needle, and the taper gives a progressively increasing aperture through which the fuel can pass. At full throttle, the needle offers virtually no obstruction to the fuel, and the amount passing through is controlled by the capacity of the main jet itself.

This arrangement gives, at least in part, the variable fuel supply that is needed. But, the air supply has to be kept in proportion. This is done by means of the throttle, which opens or closes a slide valve set in the venturi. With the throttle closed, the slide is so far down that it cuts off all but a trickle of the air supply. Opening the throttle more and more lifts the slide higher and higher, progressively increasing the amount of

The rich-mixture device on this Mikuni carburettor – used on some Suzuki and Yamaha models – is a small piston that covers and uncovers internal passages through which extra fuel is fed into the venturi

air that can pass. At full throttle, the air is flowing almost unobstructed through the venturi; only the small needle of the needle jet is in its path.

The throttle-valve arrangement is too coarse, however, to regulate the minute fuel requirements when the engine is idling. For this condition, a very fine jet known as the 'pilot' or 'slow running jet' is used to supply little more than a whiff of petrol, and usually the metered air supply is bled across the closed throttle slide to supply the necessary mixture. This air supply is controlled by the pilot air screw – a tapered needle which is set to give the correct amount of air. Its adjustment is critical, usually, to within one-eighth of a turn.

Keeping the proper fuel/air balance is controlled not only by jets, but also by the cutaway on the throttle slide. A deep cutaway admits more air than a shallow one, and the correct slide is determined at the design stage. Slide and jets have to be matched to keep in step, and all have some part of the throttle range where they are dominant. From three-quarters throttle onwards, the main jet has the most effect. For the first eighth of throttle movement, perhaps, the main jet has no effect at all and the pilot jet is in charge. On pick-up from idling, for perhaps another eighth of throttle movement, the mixture control exercised by the throttle cutaway predominates. And for half the range, the greatest single effect is that of the needle jet.

Since the needle has such a bearing on the performance of the engine, it has to be matched to the

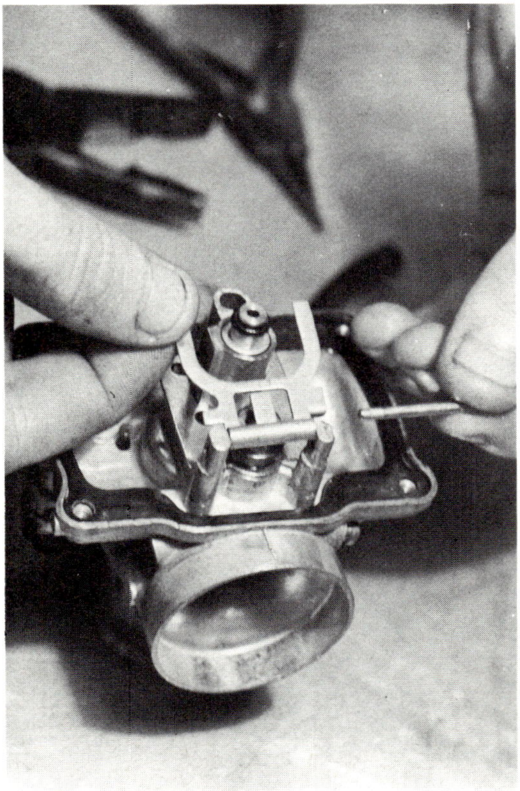

unit very carefully. Jet needles are *not* interchangeable at random! In addition, the actual position of the needle is made adjustable by using a spring clip to hold it in the throttle slide, and providing a series of mounting notches round the top of the needle so that it can be repositioned higher or lower in the slide. Usually, the needle is used with the clip in the second notch from the top, but the flow of fuel into the venturi can be varied by altering the needle setting. Using a lower notch raises the needle and gives a richer mixture. Using a higher notch lowers the needle and gives a weaker mixture.

For acceleration, even relatively simple carburettors now sometimes use power jets. All fuel fed into the venturi is drawn there by the drop in pressure caused as air flows from the higher pressure (atmospheric) side of the intake to the lower pressure (cylinder) side. The venturi itself is shaped as a double taper, so speeding the flow of air through the central section of the venturi (mixing chamber) even more. The faster the air flows through, the lower the pressure becomes, and the more rapidly the fuel is sucked up from the float chamber and through the jets.

By utilising the sudden pressure change as the throttle is opened for acceleration, an extra charge of fuel can be induced to rise through the power jet system – this is basically an auxiliary jet, with its own air supply to emulsify the mixture, and designed to feed into the airstream just forward of the venturi to give the required boost.

However, the slide-type carbu-

Top, left: the float arm on a Mikuni carburettor, showing the central tab that operates the needle valve. Bending this tab upwards or downwards will alter the fuel level in the float chamber

Top, right: most needle-valve assemblies follow this design by screwing into the carburettor body. In time, the needle becomes pitted and allows seepage, so renewal about every 15,000 miles is advisable

rettor is not always 100 per cent efficient when sudden acceleration is demanded and the throttle is snapped open. Here, the effect is to slow down the air that passes across the jet. The fuel still comes out in increased quantity, but fails to atomise properly – the droplets remain large, instead of breaking down into the fine spray that is required for combustion – and the engine hesitates momentarily before speeding up.

This fault is eradicated by use of a constant-vacuum (or constant-velocity) carburettor, which can be regarded as a more sophisticated variant of the simple slide-type instrument.

The major difference between the two is that in the CV carburettor the slide and needle are controlled automatically, while their throttle function is taken over by a simple pivoted flap, known as a butterfly, to which the rider's throttle control is linked.

The automatic control for the slide and needle is a vacuum piston. In some cases, this is suspended from a diaphragm. The upper side of the piston, or its diaphragm, is enclosed in a chamber with no outlet to the air outside, although it *is* linked – via holes in the underside of the vacuum piston – to the carburettor venturi. Its underside is open to a second chamber. This has no connection to the carburettor venturi, but is open to the outside air by way of passages formed in the air intake.

As the engine is started, the pressure in the venturi drops below that of the outside air. The vacuum chamber above the diaphragm being linked to the venturi, the pressure there drops too, while the pressure underneath the diaphragm remains the same. It therefore pushes the diaphragm upwards, lifting the slide and the needle with it. The degree of lift

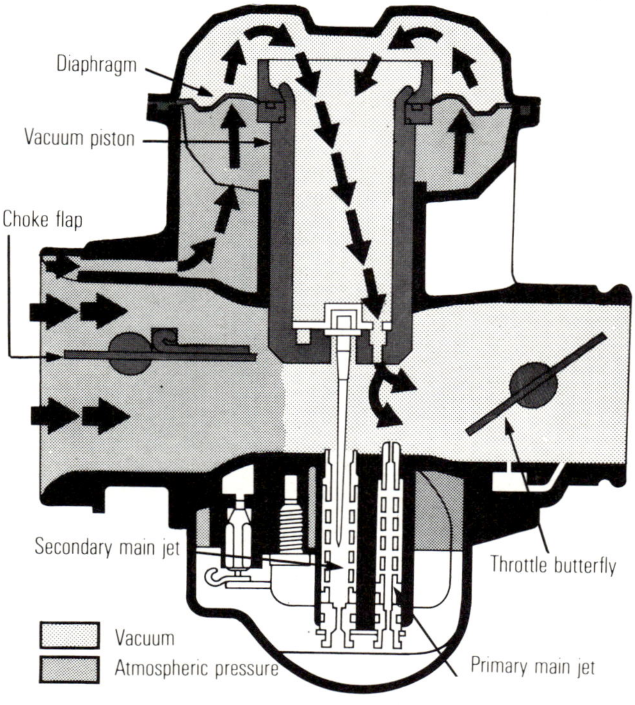

The CV carburettor (1)
This type of carburettor is now widely used as an alternative to the cable-operated throttle slide instrument, especially on bikes over 250 cc. The throttle slide (piston) is vacuum controlled and the throttle is a butterfly flap valve. In this diagram, the intake vacuum is acting on the upper side of the diaphragm through holes in the base of the piston, and atmospheric pressure on the lower side pushes the diaphragm up and raises the slide and needle

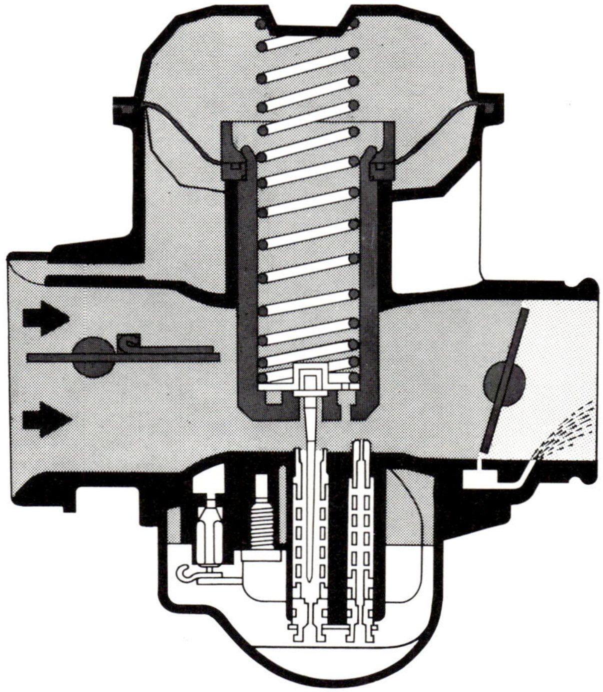

The CV carburettor (2)
At idling speed, the intake vacuum is on the engine side of throttle butterfly and the slide stays down. An idling jet behind the throttle provides the slow-running mixture

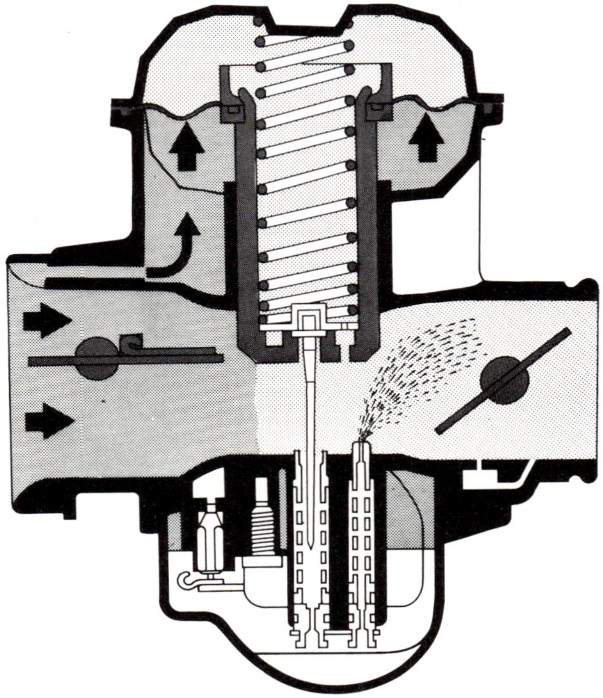

The CV carburettor (3)
As the throttle is partly opened a moderate vacuum acts on the diaphragm, so partly raising the piston. Fuel feed is mainly from the primary jet, since the needle is still restricting the main jet

The CV carburettor (4)
At full throttle, the influence of the vacuum is at maximum effect and the piston is fully raised. The needle is now clear of the main jet, and fuel spurts from both main and primary jets

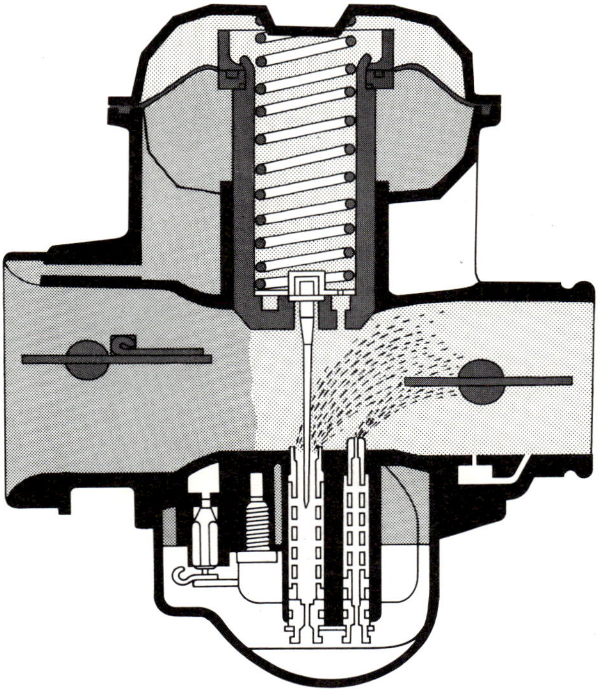

The CV carburettor (5)
Closing the choke for starting moves the vacuum forward to the choke flap. All three jets feed in fuel, and since the flap restricts the airflow the result is a rich mixture

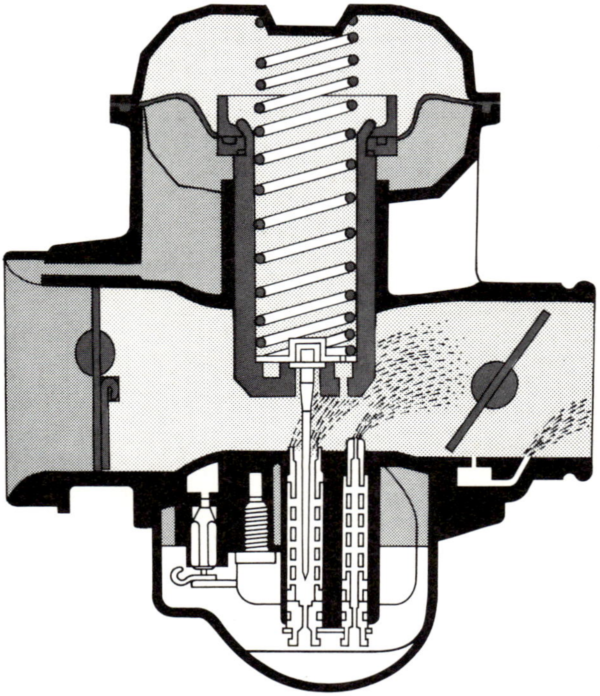

is in direct proportion to the differences in pressure, but with this system the air passing through the venturi always travels at a constant speed, although its actual volume changes. This ensures complete fuel atomisation, regardless of engine speed and throttle opening, while the vacuum that lifts the piston also draws in an extra shot of fuel from the jet to give automatic fuel enrichment at just the right moment.

Like the simple slide carburettor, the CV unit has a slow-running jet which feeds the idling mixture into the induction tract on the engine side of the butterfly. The necessary air is bled in through a small intake set just in front of the butterfly valve, which itself remains closed. As the throttle is opened, the depression in the venturi increases enough to start lifting the vacuum piston. This depression draws fuel from the main jet – usually, at this stage, from a fixed-capacity primary main jet rather than the needle-controlled secondary main jet. These two jets work in conjunction, until at full throttle the powerful intake vacuum resulting from the unrestricted airflow through the venturi has lifted the piston fully, giving a full fuel flow through both main jets.

Interestingly, when the choke (strangler) valve is being used, for starting up, the effect is to draw fuel through the two main jets as well as the pilot jet. The reason is that closing the choke valve extends the vacuum right across the venturi, so lifting the vacuum piston and opening the secondary main jet. A small flap valve formed on the choke valve is used to admit the requisite quantity of air.

Carburettor stripping

Stripping a carburettor is a straightforward job, but rebuilding it can create problems unless the precaution is taken to remove only one jet at a time so as to avoid any possibility of the jets becoming mixed up.

With the carburettor unbolted from the bike, undo the mixing chamber top and draw out the slide and needle assembly. Unless the needle has been damaged, there is no need to take it off the slide, or to remove the slide from the cable. If these operations are required, unseat the cable nipple from the slide and feed it out through its slot. The needle clip is usually positioned in the slide by a U-shaped spring. Detach the spring, and the needle/clip assembly lifts out. Older carburettors have no spring. Instead the clip passes through a slot on the upper part of the slide.

Undo the screws holding the float chamber, and pull it away from the carburettor body. It may have a gasket as a seal, or an O-ring set in a groove. O-rings can be re-used, but gaskets must always be renewed.

The most obvious component on the body is the float assembly, usually consisting of a pair of floats soldered to an arm that operates the needle valve. The pivot is a simple pin, which just pulls out. The float assembly and the needle can then be lifted out. The valve itself is screwed into the body, and has a soft-metal washer interposed. This should be renewed on assembly if the valve seat has been removed, although there is normally no need to dismantle it.

The main jet can be unscrewed for cleaning or renewal – all fuel is slightly abrasive, and a jet that has given 15,000 miles of service will almost certainly have an enlarged orifice. Jets should be cleaned only by being washed in petrol and blown clear with a blast of air applied from the side opposite to that in which the fuel normally flows. It is permissible to poke a natural bristle into the jet, but *never* a piece of wire. Even soft wire can enlarge the delicately-calibrated hole in the jet and upset the carburation.

For cleaning, the main jet is usually taken off still attached to the emulsion tube on which it is mounted, and both are washed-out together. Refit these parts first, then remove, in turn, the slow-running jet; and the power jet if fitted.

It is not normally necessary to disturb the pilot air screw but if it is removed it should be reset after the carburettor is rebuilt. In this case, the procedure is to screw it in by hand, very gently, until resistance is felt. The tapers are then in close contact, and it is important not to turn the screw any further, or the faces may be damaged. Then unscrew 1¼ turns (or whatever setting is specified for that model); final tuning is carried out when the carburettor is refitted and the engine is idling.

So far as the main body of the carburettor is concerned, there is little difference in stripping procedures between a slide-type unit and a CV carburettor. The vacuum system of the CV instrument is a little more complicated. After detaching the top of the chamber, the slide return spring is removed, followed by the piston and diaphragm which are usually combined in one unit. The only part which can be renewed separately is the needle, which is retained in the piston either by a screw or clip fixing.

CV carburettors that use only a vacuum piston and no diaphragm are basically similar in construction, but have seals on the piston and, also, usually a slot and guide screw to position it in the carburettor body to prevent it turning.

CV instruments have a wear-point not shared with slide carburettors. After a very high mileage, the pivot holes for the throttle butterfly may wear oval and cause an air leakage which will upset the carburation. With this fault, a new carburettor body is required, unless it is possible to drill and rebush the hole to take a new standard-size spindle.

Balancing multi carburettors on modern four-cylinder bikes demands a nest of four vacuum gauges to ensure that each carburettor is synchronised with its neighbour. One gauge is linked to a take-off point on each induction tract, and with the engine set at 2,000 rpm a check is made to ensure that each gives the same reading. If not, the settings on one or more cylinders are varied until all the readings tally. It is basically a matter of setting the throttle opening on each carburettor linkage to get the same speed – more fiddly than difficult.

With twin-carburettor layouts, the problem is halved, and a skilled mechanic can often synchronise the carburettors with a length of plastic tubing. With the air filters disconnected, he listens to the hiss of air entering each venturi, using the tubing as a form of stethoscope. When he has obtained the same degree of hiss from each carburettor by adjusting the throttle screws, he knows they are synchronised.

Balancing devices in which suction causes a tell-tale ball to rise in a tube perform the same function, only visually.

As an aid to obtaining the correct mixture setting, a device called a Colortune can be used. This is basically a sparking plug with a transparent top that enables the flame conditions in the combustion chamber to be seen. With the Colortune fitted in place of the standard plug and the engine idling, the colour of the combustion flame is noted. The correct mixture burns with a bright 'Bunsen blue' flame. Weak mixtures give a whitish tinge, rich ones a yellowish colour. Adjustment for correct mixture is usually carried out by means of the pilot air screw(s). On CV instruments, turning the jet stop nut downwards gives an enriched mixture, and vice versa.

Fuel filters

Filtration of both air and fuel is normal practice on motorcycles. Most fuel filters are of simple mesh design, designed to trap any flecks of dirt that are large enough to block a jet. To take account of smaller particles that pass through the mesh, the float chamber is usually equipped with a well at the bottom to form a sludge trap. This gathers quite a deposit of dirt in the course of time, together with any water that has entered the fuel. Periodically, therefore, the chamber should be removed for cleaning, unless it is fitted with a drain screw. In this case, the screw is removed and the fuel tap turned on for a second or two to flush. Some carburettors have a taper screw linking to the overflow system.

The fuel tap usually has a mesh-type filter surrounding its pick-ups, and this should be removed once a year for cleaning, the tank having first been allowed to run dry. Some fuel will still be trapped in the bottom, but this again is likely to be fouled by dirt and water. The tank should be flushed with clean petrol, and the filter washed in petrol and gently scrubbed with a stiff brush. An old toothbrush is ideal.

The carburettor filter is invariably mounted in the inlet union so as to filter the fuel before it reaches the needle valve. It is cleaned in a similar manner to the tap filter.

Some fuel taps have a built-in sludge trap in the form of a miniature bowl into which the impurities fall as the fuel flows into the fuel line through a mesh filter. The bowl should be removed and flushed out periodically. Some machines, too, have an in-line mesh filter inserted into the pipe from the tank to the float chamber. This type, inherited from automobile practice, is a sealed filter which is discarded at intervals and replaced by a new one.

Air filters

Air filters are either paper-element 'dry' units, or oil-wetted sponge. The dry element is cleaned by removing it from the filter housing, tapping it hard against a wall to loosen the surface dirt, and then blowing it clean with an air line. In the course of time, however, the element becomes impregnated with dirt which cannot be removed. For this reason the element should be renewed at the intervals specified in the manufacturer's handbook.

Oil-wetted filters trap the dirt in the induced air as it passes through a relatively coarse foam whose interstices are loaded with engine oil. The dirt sticks to the oil, and is retained inside the foam. To clean this type of filter, remove the foam 'element' – usually a strip – and wash it thoroughly in petrol. After hanging it up to dry, dip the element in clean oil and allow to drain before refitting.

Both types of air filter form a partial obstruction to the airflow, and there is sometimes a temptation to remove them in a search for more power. The result is rarely worthwhile – internal wear in the engine and carburettor is greatly increased by the thousands of small but very hard and abrasive particles which the air contains – and unless the carburation is reset to compensate for the greater flow of air, the result is a weak mixture and engine overheating.

Ignition and electrical equipment

Since the sole object of a motorcycle ignition system is to make a high-voltage spark jump across the points of a sparking plug, we will first examine the role of the humble and familiar plug.

Sparking plug

At first glance, the job of a sparking plug looks a sinecure. It is screwed into the cylinder head, with its nose in the combustion chamber, and only has to provide a spark at most once in every revolution of the crank. However, this is not the case, since the voltage needed to produce the spark is a minimum of 14,000 volts – getting on for that carried in the National Grid! – while the temperature in the cylinder, once the mixture ignites, is of blowtorch intensity.

A typical sparking plug comprises a metal body, a ceramic insulator, a central electrode passing through the insulator, and a side electrode fixed to the body. These electrodes are usually made of specially-formulated steel, although sometimes gold-palladium or platinum are used instead to allow electrodes to be thinner. These hotter-running types burn off deposits more easily, and so are more resistant to fouling. Some types of plug have part of the centre electrode fabricated from a copper alloy instead of steel. This helps the internal heat distribution. Other plugs have a built-in auxiliary gap across which the current has to jump before it reaches the points gap. This boosts the voltage at the plug points – most experienced riders know that a fouled plug can often be cleared by holding the cap a few millimetres from the terminal, and jumping a spark across it. Built-in spark gaps are a scientific way of doing the same thing.

Each plug on the market has been designed to work within a specific heat range, which is determined by the amount of heat the plug can pass on to the surrounding metal of the cylinder head and how much it retains within itself. A 'cold' plug – sometimes called a 'hard' plug – has a relatively short nose exposed to the combustion gases and consequently absorbs less heat into itself. It is thus relatively cool running, which means that it has less ability to burn off deposits. Used in a cool-running engine, or one that burns oil, the 'cold' plug would soon foul up. 'Cold' plugs, therefore, are used for high-performance, highly-stressed engines.

In a 'hot' or 'soft' plug the insulator nose is longer, so that the plug itself absorbs more heat and transfers less. Consequently, it has the ability to burn off deposits, and is used in a cool-running engine. A hot plug should never be used in a hot-running, highly-stressed engine as it could absorb so much heat that its end would melt. Before this happened, it would start to act as a glow-plug, prematurely igniting the

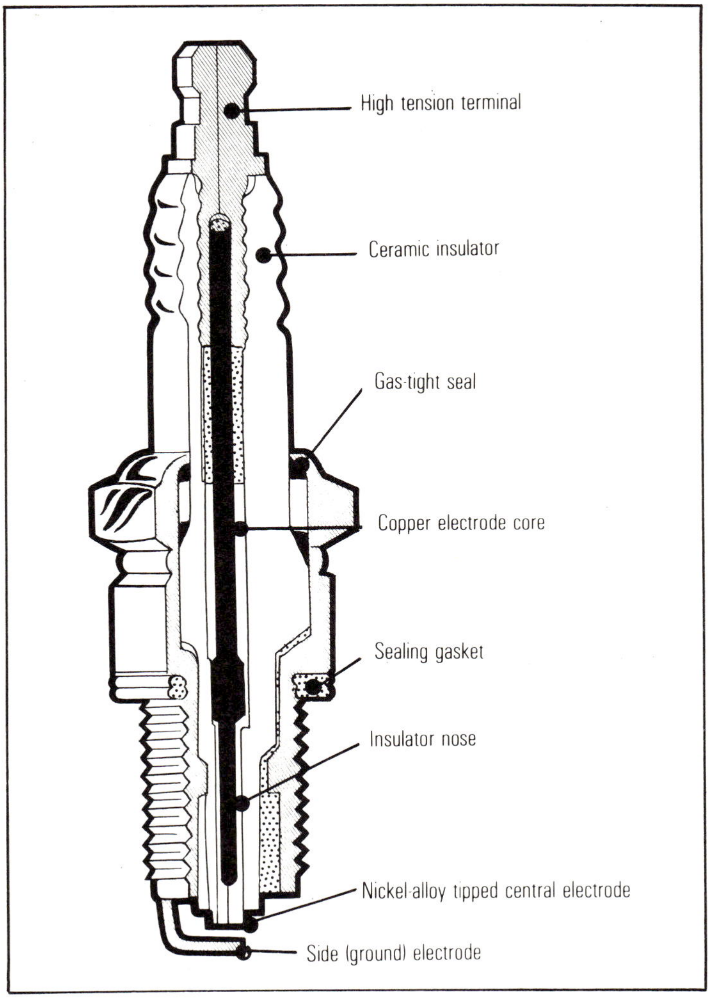

The modern sparking plug is complex, but cheap and reliable – the result of 80 years' development

mixture by virtue of its heat alone, and so causing the engine to 'pink'. In extreme cases, the heat build-up could become so intense, locally, that a hole would be burnt through the piston crown.

Sparking plugs are currently made mainly in three sizes: 10 mm, for use where space for a plug hole is limited; an intermediate 12 mm size; and the more popular 14 mm. A number of old engines require 18 mm plugs.

A second dimension applied to a plug is its 'reach' – the length of the threaded portion. The longer the reach, the greater the projection into the plug hole. Fitting a long-reach plug in a head designed for a short-reach one may result in the plug being struck by the piston, with obvious results!

Plug faults normally show up under acceleration or when higher speeds are being maintained. The reason is that the voltage needed to send a spark across the electrodes rises as the working conditions become more arduous. Where 5,000 volts may be adequate with the bike being cruised gently, with new plugs, the same speed with worn plugs may demand 10,000 volts. Accelerating

Right: the basis of the ignition system. Electrical current passed through a straight cable produces a weak, tube-like magnetic field round the outside

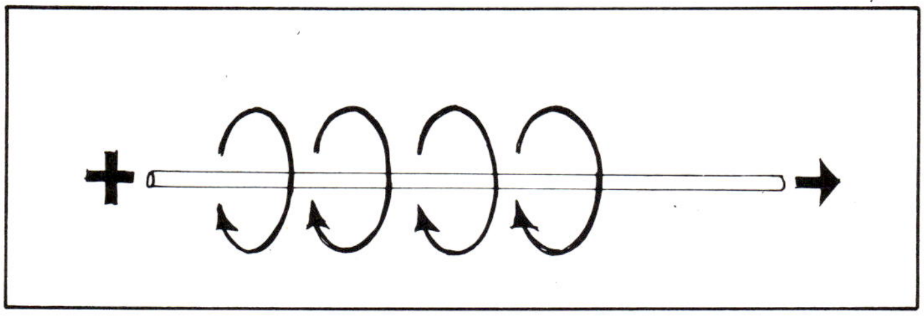

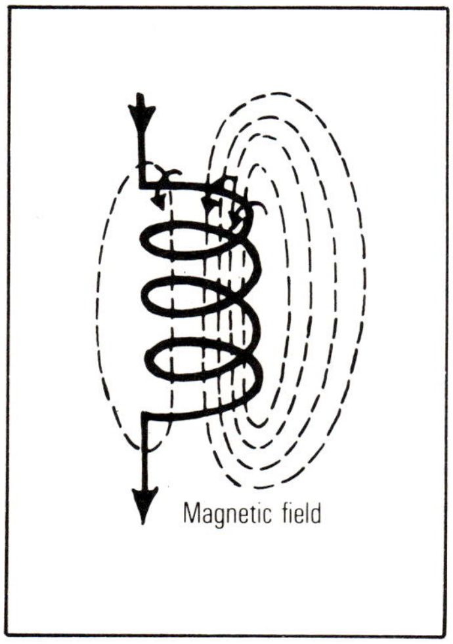

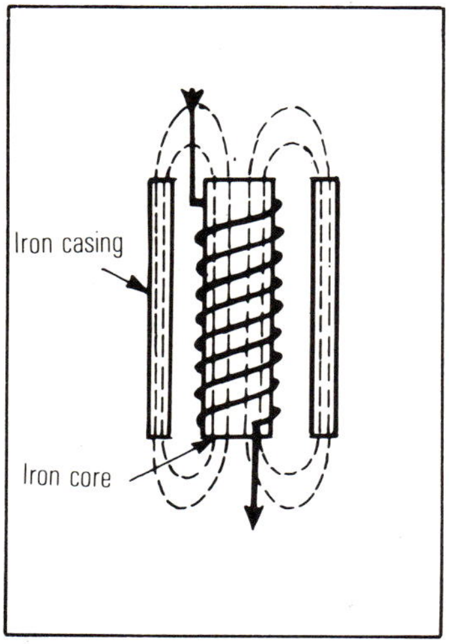

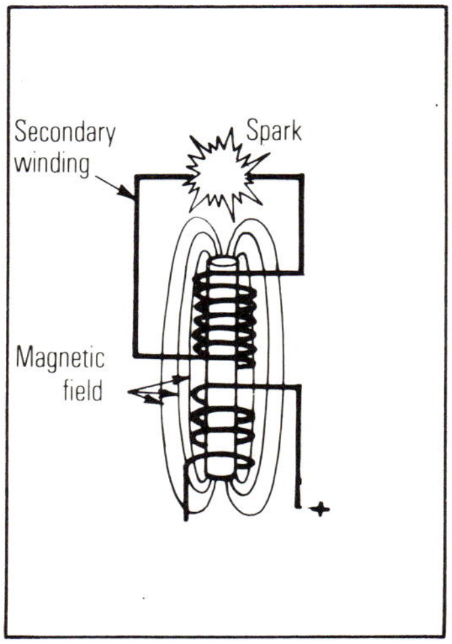

Above: this principle is extended by coiling the cable. Now the magnetic lines of force intersect to produce a bigger and much stronger magnetic field

Above, centre: yet another step. Placing a soft-iron core within the coiled cable, and enclosing it in an iron casing, makes the field stronger still. This is the basis of an ignition coil

Above, right: why a coil anyway? This is how it makes a spark at the plug points. Low-voltage current is supplied to the primary winding, and then suddenly switched off. The magnetic field collapses, and this causes a pulse of high-voltage current to be induced in the secondary winding

hard, the new plugs could demand 16,000 volts – the worn ones 25,000 volts. Since the average ignition system produces only about 20,000 volts, the result is immediate misfiring.

The condition of the firing end of the plug provides evidence of the state of the engine in which it has been running. Normal running results in an insulator that is a light coffee colour, with perhaps a trace of grey on the tip. A build-up of light-coloured, rather chalky, ash indicates that the plug needs cleaning, but is otherwise satisfactory for further use. A light-coloured insulator tip coupled with excessive wear on the electrodes means that the plug is running too hot, and may indicate a need for a slightly colder plug grade. A whitish or grey nose means a weak mixture.

Where the insulator nose is sooted-up with soft, black carbon, this indicates an over-rich setting of the fuel mixture. The nose of an oil-fouled plug is also black, but is hard and scaly. There is another type of fouling that shows you are spending good money to no effect – lead fouling. A lead-fouled plug, usually associated with misfiring, may have a nose colour varying from dark grey to green. It means that the petrol in your tank is of too high an octane rating for your motor – such as using four-star fuel, when the bike's manufacturers designed it to run on two-star. You get no extra performance – just fouled plugs and extra expense.

Ignition coil and contact breaker

We have seen that to produce a spark at the plug points it is necessary to feed in the sort of voltage normally associated with power stations rather than motor-

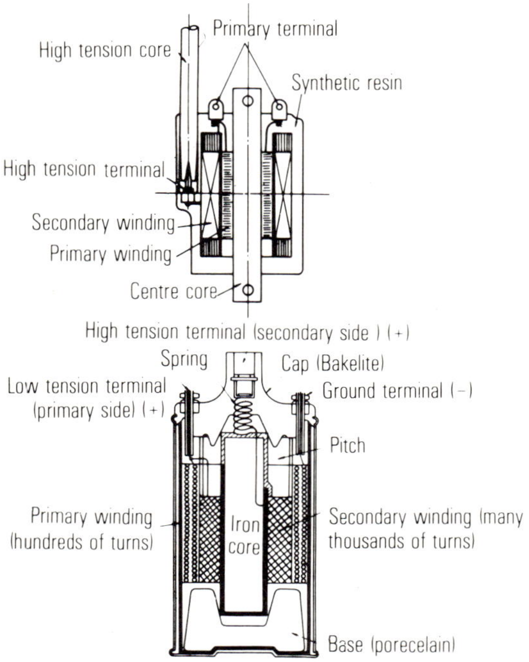

And here is the ignition coil itself – in two versions.

Top: This is the more modern moulded coil which has the primary windings inside the secondary windings. The moulded coil is more resistant to vibration and is now extensively used on motorcycles

Below: this cannister type coil has the primary windings carried round the outside of the secondary windings

cycles. Since the bike's electrical system relies mainly on a 12-volt battery, how is this seeming miracle worked?

The answer lies, basically, in two components – the ignition coil, and the contact-breaker mechanism: although the latter is now often superseded by electronic triggering.

The theory behind the coil is simple enough – an electrical current flowing through a straight piece of wire creates a small magnetic field that rotates round the outside of the conductor. Form the wire into a coil instead, pass the same current through it, and the lines of force of the magnetic field merge. Result? A bigger and more powerful field, which can be strengthened even more if a soft iron core is used in the middle of the coil, and an iron casing is placed around the outside. This is an electro-magnet.

If the magnetic field can be rapidly collapsed, by suddenly cutting off the current that produces it, the effect is to produce a pulse of high-voltage electricity in the coil. The voltage is in direct proportion to the number of turns of wire in the coil – the more turns the greater the voltage.

Ignition coils for motorcycles are really double coils. One – called the primary winding – carries the current fed by the battery. This winding comprises a few hundred turns of thick wire. Within this coil is a second one, called the secondary winding. This is made up of many thousands of turns of thin enamelled wire. One end of this winding connects to the centre electrode of the plug; the other to the electrode on the plug body, which is effectively 'earthed' to the frame of the bike.

Interrupting the low-voltage electrical current in the primary

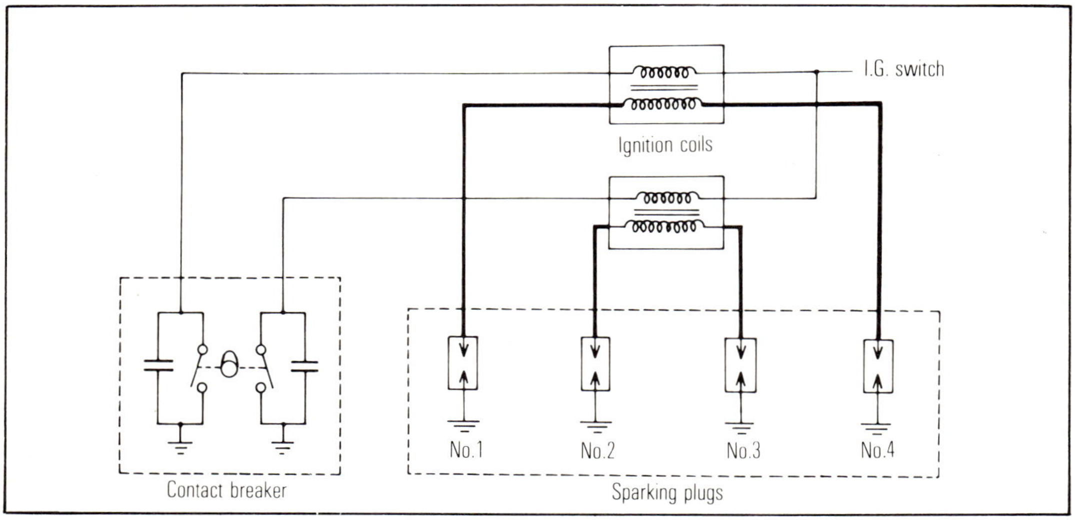

Above: in this ignition system used on the Suzuki GS750 'four', the twin contact breakers are operated at crankshaft speed. This produces twice as many sparks as the motor really needs. Cylinders Nos. 1 and 4 fire simultaneously, and so do cylinders 2 and 3. However, only one of each pair is on the compression stroke, and the 'spare' spark takes place at the top of the exhaust stroke in the other, where it has no practical effect

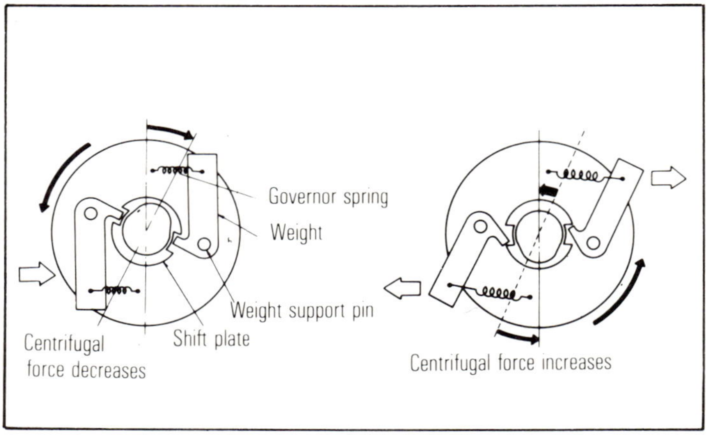

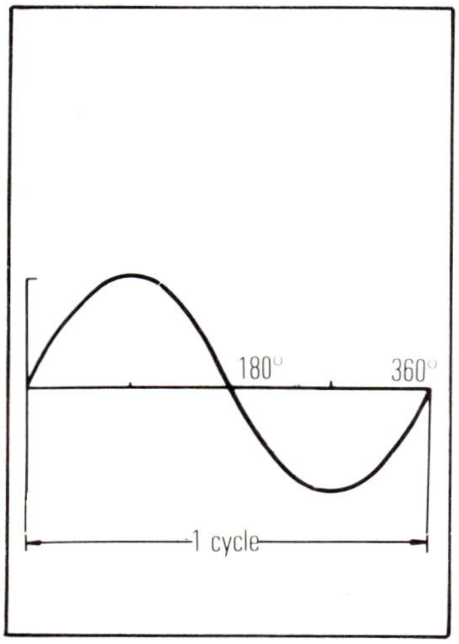

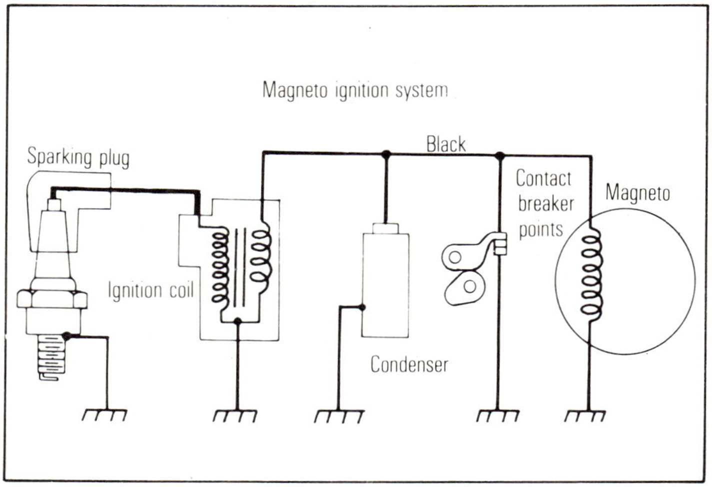

winding produces a collapse of the magnetic field and induces a current of perhaps 300 volts, but in the closely-wound secondary winding this is boosted to 14,000 volts or more. This is the current that jumps the gap between the plug electrodes in the form of a fat blue spark, and ignites the compressed mixture in the combustion chamber.

The mechanical switch that produces the spark – the contact breaker – is also used to ensure that the spark occurs at just the right moment. It has to be timed to occur while the piston is still rising, but is almost at the top of its stroke. That gives the mixture a millisecond or so in which to ignite, and to burn at full intensity to thrust the piston down as it passes TDC. The contact breaker comprises one contact point carried on a pivoted arm, which is operated by a cam, and a second point which is fixed. Current flows through the points from the battery via the primary winding. The cam is driven by the crankshaft, at engine speed for two-strokes and usually at half-engine speed for four-strokes. As the cam lifts the pivoted arm it breaks the primary circuit – and the result is that a high voltage (HT) spark is produced at the plug points.

The contact-breaker points, which are made of platinum, would rapidly be eroded by arcing occurring between them caused by the voltage generated by the collapse of the primary circuit magnetic field, were no 'shock absorber' incorporated. This is the role of the condensor – which is an electrical storehouse connected across the contact breaker. Its job is to soak up the pulse of current from the primary circuit that would otherwise try to jump the gap between the contact-breaker points. Instead, as the points open, the pulse enters the condensor. With no current flowing through the primary winding, there is a path back to earth through the ignition switch and across the battery, and this is the route taken by the pulse. In doing so, it actually helps to collapse the coil's magnetic field, and so produces an even fatter spark at the plug points.

On four-stroke units, it is usual to incorporate a mechanical system for advancing and retarding the timing of the spark. Many modern four-stroke units solve the problem of needing to run the contact-breaker at half engine speed by driving it direct from the crankshaft, in the same way as a two-stroke. This results in twice as many sparks as are actually needed, the plug firing at TDC on both the compression and exhaust strokes. Obviously, this 'stray' spark has no practical effect.

With four-strokes, however, it is desirable to match the timing of the spark to the travel of the piston, and this means adapting it to the engine speed. If the engine is to develop maximum power, the thrust must be applied to the piston just as it passes the top of its stroke and starts to descend. The petrol/air mixture takes a split second to reach maximum burning rate: therefore, it has to be ignited a little early. Advancing the spark to provide this earlier combustion is achieved by making the contact-breaker cam a loose twist fit on the end of its driving shaft, and using weights to alter the relative position of the shaft and the cam. The faster the engine revolves, the further the weights fly out. In doing so, they twist the cam round the shaft against the direction of rotation, so advancing the ignition. As the engine slows, the springs that restrain the weights take over and pull them back. That twists the cam in the same direction as the rotation of the shaft, and makes the spark occur later.

Opposite, centre: Four-stroke engines usually have the ignition timing automatically varied, so allowing the spark to occur earlier as the engine speed rises. This is done by mounting the contact-breaker cam so that it is free to move on its shaft, under the control of centrifugal weights. At low speeds (*left-hand diagram*) the weights are held retracted by a pair of springs and the cam is in such a position relative to the shaft that it gives the spark at the correct time for idling. As the engine is speeded up, the weights begin to fly outwards, twising the cam on the shaft and steadily advancing the ignition timing

Opposite, lower left: for the primary windings of the coil, direct current is needed. Magnetos and alternators, however, produce alternating current, with positive and negative pulses, as in this wave. Only the positive pulse is required

Opposite, lower right: the Kawasaki magneto ignition system designed to use only half of the current wave. The contact breaker points stay closed while the useless negative wave is being generated, feeding it straight to earth. The points open for the positive wave, sending it on to the primary windings, and then close again to earth the supply and to collapse the magnetic field.

With this type of ignition system, the setting of the points is critical for maximum efficiency

While two-stroke engines have fixed ignition timings, most four-strokes have a device similar to this for varying the point at which the spark occurs. It is a centrifugal advance/ retard mechanism, in which movement outwards of the spring-loaded weights rotates the cam that operates the contact-breaker points

Removal of the mechanism discloses that the cam is a sliding fit on the shaft. If this mechanism is dismantled, it is essential not to stretch the springs, whose tension is critical to its operation

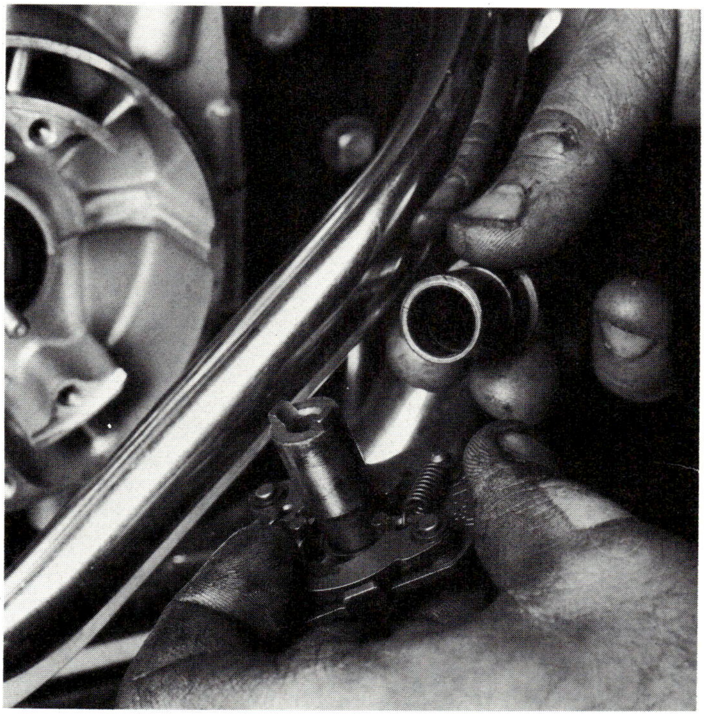

Magneto ignition

So far, we have dealt with the most numerically-popular ignition circuit in which the primary low-tension (LT) current is supplied by a 12 volt, or even a 6 volt, battery. In the smaller capacity classes, though, there is an alternative ignition system known as the flywheel magneto.

A magneto consists of a number of coils set inside a rotating magnet. Normally, a pair of magnets are set into the periphery of a flywheel, and revolve around the coils.

Like all magnets, these have North and South poles. As each magnet passes a coil, it causes an electrical current to flow in the windings. Current produced by a North Pole magnet flows one way: that produced by a South Pole magnet flows in the other direction. The result is the generation of alternating current (AC), as opposed to direct current (DC) which is supplied by a battery.

The ignition coil will not function on alternating current – the primary winding must be fed with DC. Alternating current can be regarded as a wave, with a peak and a trough set equally above a median line, and for AC to be used, the contact breaker is so arranged that it selects a single positive wave to feed the primary windings. It works – but the current pulse is available for little more than 60° of crankshaft rotation, so accurate points setting with this system is of prime importance. With a magneto system, pulses are induced as the flywheel turns, but while the contact-breaker points are closed they pass straight to earth. Current does not flow to the primary winding until the points open, where it then sets up a magnetic field in the windings. The points remain open until the positive pulse reaches a peak, when they are arranged to close. That earths the generated LT current and in the coil, with the supply cut off, the magnetic field collapses to generate the HT current.

While the contact-breaker system works reliably and well, it has its mechanical limits. The points opening is positive: but their return is by springs, and when rotational speeds become too great the system is unable to react quickly enough, and the points simply bounce. This mechanical limit is reached at around 10,000 switchings per minute. Above that speed, the points oscillate; the necessary HT current cannot be produced; and power falls off.

This means that the maximum rotational speed of a petrol engine is governed by the ability of the contact breaker to respond. The answer to this problem was to dispense with the contact breaker, and to utilise electronics to break the circuit instead.

Transistorised ignition system

A typical transistorised ignition system is that used by Yamaha, where a two-pole magneto produces a single cycle of alternating current to each complete revolution of the crankshaft. Two coils are used, stationed 180° apart, at the edge of the rotor. That on the left is a pulse coil, whose sole job is to signal when the spark is due. That on the right is the charge coil, which produces current. This current, however, is not fed directly into the circuit. Instead, it charges up a condensor.

In the circuit are solid-state electronic 'valves' known as diodes and thyristors. The diodes allow current to pass in only one direction: the thyristor allows it to pass in one direction too, but only after it has itself been switched on.

As the rotor turns, its timing mark passes the charge coil. This

Diagram of Yamaha's capacitor discharge ignition system (CDI), designed to cope with engine speeds beyond the limitations of mechanical contact breakers. Diodes and a thyristor are used to switch the primary circuit.

The operational sequence is that a pulse coil is used to signal when the spark is due; a charge coil produces a current which is stored in a condensor; and the thyristor releases the current at the designed moment

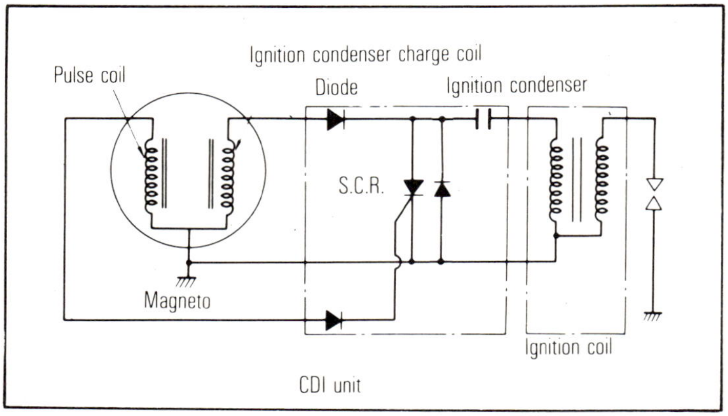

The first stage . . . a charge of alternating current from the generator is sent towards the ignition condenser (capacitor). A diode inserted in the line, however, rejects the negative pulses, allowing only the positive pulses to pass through

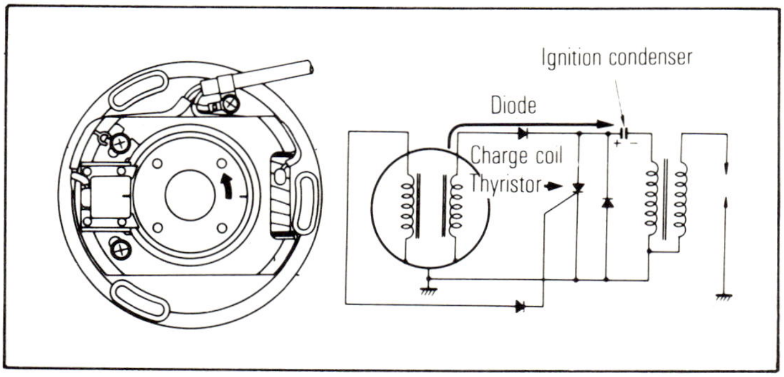

The generator rotor has now turned through 180°, and the timing mark has aligned with the pulse coil. This produces a pulse of current, which is fed to the thyristor gate to signal that the spark should now be made

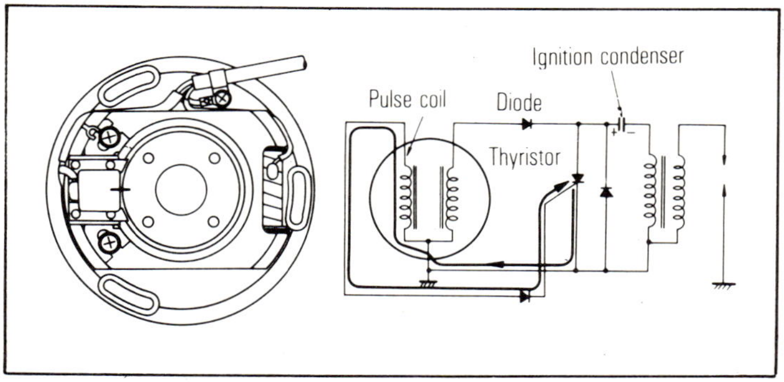

The response is instantaneous, since electricity travels at 186,000 miles per second! The pulse makes the thyristor conductive, and the current stored in the ignition condensor therefore streaks out through it and into the primary windings of the ignition coil. Current flow is limited to the amount stored in the capacitor. Cessation of this current flow causes the magnetic field to collapse, generating HT current in the secondary windings in the normal way, and producing a spark at the plug points

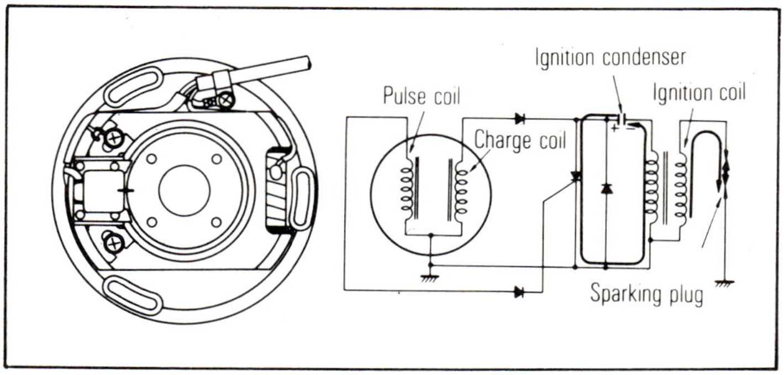

feeds high-voltage direct current into the condensor, where it is stored. It is direct current because only one half of the AC wave has been allowed through the upper diode. The lower half of the wave has been rejected. The rotor continues to turn until the point at which the spark is needed is reached. A second pulse of current is then fed through – this time, to the thyristor. This switches the thryistor, which in turn releases not the wave fed to it, but the current stored in the condensor. This flows through the primary windings, and produces the HT current needed by the plug.

With no mechanical restrictions imposed upon it, this transistorised ignition system is capable of operating reliably at the highest speeds of which a piston engine is capable – and it never needs servicing.

Battery

The coil ignition system, whether it is operated by the conventional contact breaker or by electronics, is dependent upon the battery to provide the initial low-tension current.

In general terms, a battery consists of a series of plates immersed in acid. The basis of the battery is the cell – each of which is rated at two volts. A 12-volt battery therefore consists of six two-volt cells.

The plates are arranged in pairs – a positive plate and a negative plate. Each working plate comprises a framework and a grid of antimony-lead alloy. Positive plates have this grid filled with a paste made of lead particles, lead oxide, and sulphuric acid. This paste is dried, and chemically processed to transform it into lead peroxide. This active material is anchored by matting made of superfine glass fibres of between five and 30 microns diameter.

Built on a similar grid, the negative plate is coated with spongy lead which has no positive locator. The positive and negative plates are, however, separated by a shield of synthetic resin or porous ebonite. A series of plates and separators is immersed in an electrolyte solution composed of sulphuric acid and distilled water with a specific gravity of 1·260–1·280, and the plates are linked to common terminals – positive plates to a positive terminal; negative plates to a negative terminal.

Before use, the cells that comprise the battery are charged. When the terminals are linked – as when switching on a headlamp, for example – the effect is to draw electrical current from the cell. This current is provided by the chemical change taking place within the cell itself.

As the cell discharges, the interaction between the lead peroxide, the spongy lead, and the sulphuric acid causes the active ingredients on both positive and negative plates to turn into lead sulphate. To do this, they draw on the sulphur content of the acid. As the battery runs down, therefore, the acid becomes more and more diluted, until at a specific gravity of 1·220 it is fully discharged.

Batteries are rated by the amperage they can deliver over a set time. Thus a 20 ah (ampere-hour) battery could, in theory, deliver one amp for 20 hours, or 20 amps for one hour.

Battery maintenance. – To prolong the life of a battery, the level of the electrolyte in the battery cells should be periodically checked. In all types of battery, the electrolyte should cover the tops of the plate separators in each cell. If the level in any cell is below this, distilled water should be added to the electrolyte until the separators are covered.

The battery top must also be

Modern batteries are absolutely reliable, providing they receive a minimum of care. It is essential, for example, to clean the terminal faces back to bright metal, and then to protect them with a smear of Vaseline. This ensures there is no loss of current due to resistance at the terminals

kept clean and dry and the cable connectors should fit tightly. Failure of an engine to start or continue to run can often be traced to loose or dirty battery connections, and it may be necessary to scrape the posts and the insides of the connectors to restore adequate contact.

Alternator

We have already noted how electricity is generated, and that alternating current has to be changed to direct current if it is to charge a battery. Producing the current is the job of the alternator; changing it to DC and controlling the output requires sophisticated electronics.

The direction of the pulses of alternating current change according to the position of the north and south poles of the generator rotor relative to the coils. Adding a single diode into the circuit allows pulses travelling in one direction to pass, but blocks the others. It works – although it wastes half the output of the generator – and this system is known as 'half wave rectification'.

By using four diodes instead of one, however, the pulses can be shunted around a circuit in such a way that they all end up going in the same direction. This 'full wave rectification' is the basis of most modern motorcycle electrical systems.

Control systems can be equally complex. The simplest is to link some of the generator coils to the light switch in such a way that only one out of, say, three is used until the lights are on, when all the rest come into play. The coil that is in constant use is connected to the battery to provide charging so long as the engine is running. One snag here is that the permanently-connected coil is under no control at all, and its charging rate can therefore be higher than

the battery needs, or less, and there is little to be done about it.

The addition of a Zener diode solves some of the problems. An ordinary diode is basically a one-way valve. A Zener diode, however, does permit current to start passing in the opposite direction once its pressure reaches 14 volts, and at 15 volts the diode has become fully conductive. Drop the pressure back below 14 volts, however, and it reverts to accepting current in one direction only.

This characteristic is used to regulate the current flow. The Zener diode is built into the charging circuit in parallel with the battery, and so long as the current being fed to the battery does not exceed 14 volts the Zener diode acts as an insulator and will not pass it into the part of the circuit that by-passes the battery. Once the voltage exceeds 14, the Zener diode starts to turn into a conductor, bleeding off part of the current so that the battery never receives more than the 14 volts it requires.

For high outputs, the simple permanent-magnet alternator is not powerful enough, so an electro-magnetic type is used instead. Basically, an electro-magnet comprises a soft iron core surrounded by coils of wire. Current passed through the wire magnetises the core. Utilise a number of such electro-magnets in the rotor, and the result is a very powerful alternator, whose output can be closely controlled by varying the current supplied to it.

Such alternators can be battery-excited or self-excited – in other words, the necessary current can be fed to the coils in the rotor direct from the bike's battery; or, the rotor itself can be tapped to do the job.

The battery-excited type is used in conjunction with a bridge of six diodes to rectify the current.

Regular checking of the electrolyte level is another essential maintenance job. It must be between the marks on the battery case. The state of charge can be checked with a hydrometer, and if the battery needs charging, it can be carried out overnight using a small home charger such as this. When charging a battery, and when installing it on the bike, ensure that the vent pipe is unkinked and free from blockage, however, or internal gassing may crack the case wide open

The stator windings are so arranged that the output of its three coils overlaps; an arrangement that produces more power in a smoother flow. This system is known as 'three-phase'. The circuit includes a relay to break the exciter circuit when the ignition is switched off, and so prevent the battery draining itself through the convenient path to earth presented by the exciter circuit.

Self-excited systems need extra diodes – to rectify the current being fed back into the generator rotor – and it is usual for nine to be used in all. With no exciter circuit to the battery to worry about, however, this type of alternator dispenses with the relay. Only a small current has to be bled off the rotor as it turns when the starter is operated, and this passes to it via the generator warning lamp. The light glows until the alternator produces enough current to equalise the voltage each side of the lamp. Equal voltage means no current flow, and the light then goes out.

Self-exciting alternators cannot be left to get *too* excited! The faster the rotor turns the more current it produces. In turn, more current is fed to the windings and this increases the output more and more. Without an external control, this power generation game could get out of hand and end up by burning out the alternator completely.

The answer lies in the voltage regulator – nowadays, usually transistorised – which holds the voltage of the generator down to 14/15 volts. An alternative is a magnetic regulator, which does the same job by use of small electro-magnets. Neither unit lends itself to do-it-yourself work. Substitution is the only practical course in the event of failure, and apart from renewing brushes on some types of alternator and battery maintenance, no other servicing should be attempted in the charging system.

Instruments

The speedometer and rev counter also work on electro-magnetic principles – eddy currents, in this case. Basically, the needle that indicates the speed of the bike or the number of rotations the crankshaft makes per minute is mounted on a disc that is induced to follow a rotating magnet. A hair spring restrains the disc, turning the unit into what is virtually a small electro-magnetic slipping clutch.

The only parts amenable to servicing are the flexible drives. These should be removed from time to time, wiped, and lubricated with grease. Oil must never be used, since the rotating drive would tend to pump it into the instrument. The lubricant is retained by the plastic sheathing round the spiral-wound outer cable. This sheathing frequently suffers damage – the cables tend to be snagged under tanks or around frame members – and any such damage should be made good with heavy-duty insulating tape to prevent loss of lubricant.

Instruments such as these are also vibration-prone (vibration spells disaster to a permanent magnet), and they must therefore be carefully rubber-mounted. Fitting the speedo and rev counter rigidly into a non-standard housing – when using a fairing, for instance – can cause rapid failure either through decomposition of the magnets, or from failure of the hair spring through fatigue.

Lights

The bulbs upon which a biker depends to light his way at night; to be seen by both pedestrians and other road users; or signal his intentions; all have a limited 'life'.

A bulb works by the passage of an electric current through a very fine wire – a filament – made from tungsten.

This small coil of highly heat-resistant wire is enclosed in a glass envelope filled with a mixture of gases – argon, krypton, and nitrogen. In air, the filament would burn out. In these inert gases, it glows white hot to produce light.

Most motorcycle bulbs are of this tungsten type, but for headlamps the halogen bulb has been developed to give a more brilliant light output (earlier names for this type of bulb were: iodine vapour, quartz iodine or quartz halogen). In these bulbs, a halogen compound, such as iodine or bromine is added to the inert gas.

The greater light output of a halogen bulb is obtained by using a higher filament temperature and a higher gas pressure within the envelope. To withstand the higher temperature and pressure, the envelope is constructed from quartz, which is much stronger than glass.

In action, the halogen gases and the tungsten filament participate in a complex chemical reaction. After reaching its working temperature, the filament starts to radiate tungsten atoms. If this was not compensated for, it would soon self-destruct – this is the reason for the halogen compound being mixed with the inert gas. The tungsten atoms from the filament impinge on the hot envelope, where they combine with

When renewing bulbs, take care not to touch the inside surface of the lamp reflector with your fingers. It can damage the sensitive silvering. If a quartz-halogen bulb is being fitted, the glass envelope should not be handled either, since grease from your skin applied to the bulb will cause a hot-spot when the lamp is on, causing it to blacken and burn

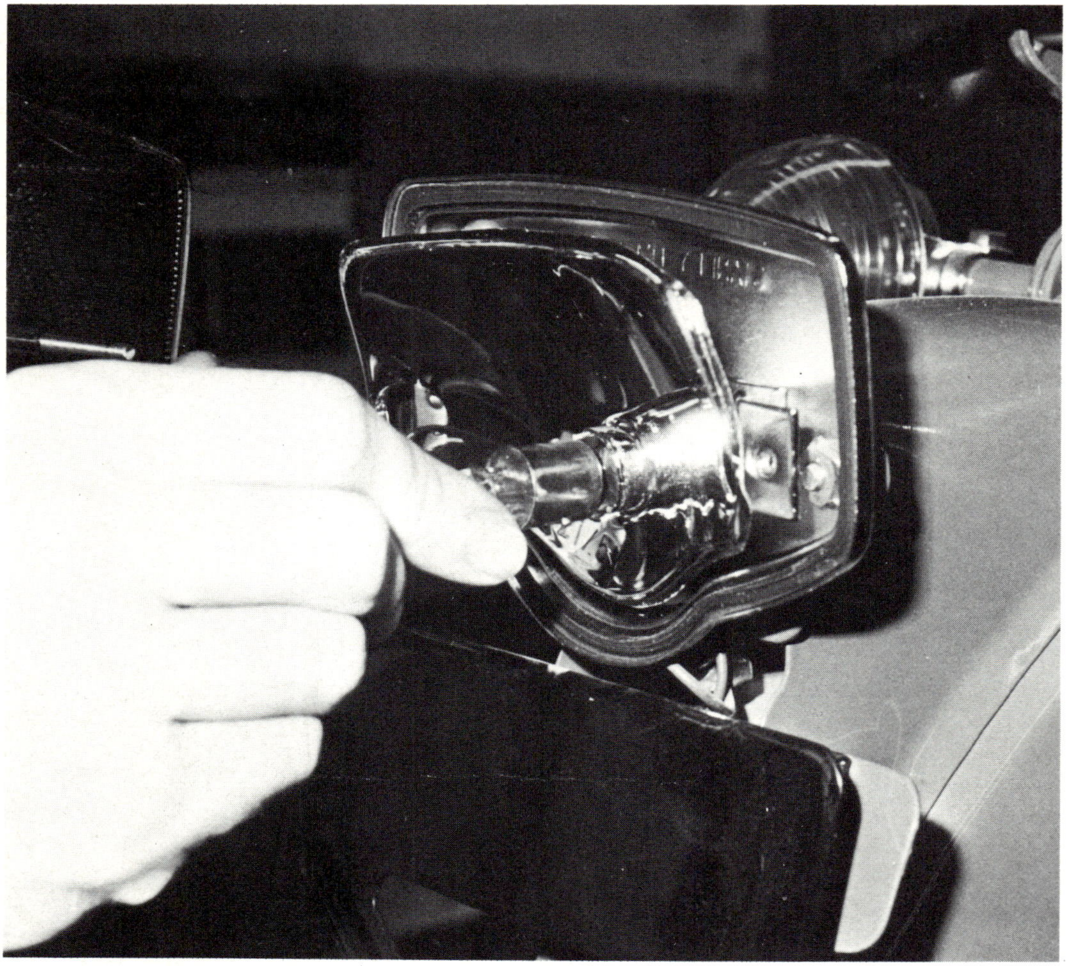

Bayonet-fitting bulbs sometimes stick in their holders if they have become surface-corroded. Too much pressure can rip the glass envelope from the bulb, or splinter it. With stubborn bulbs, wrap one or two turns of adhesive tape round the envelope before trying to turn it. A shot of WD40 often helps, too

halogen atoms from the gas. The product is a gas formed of tungsten/halogen molecules, which is unstable. Impinging on the filament, the gas breaks down again, coating the filament with the very tungsten atoms it has been discharging and liberating halogen vapour to keep the cycle going.

There is an important precaution to be taken when changing a halogen bulb. Since any grease deposited on the quartz envelope will cause localised superheating which will permanently fog the quartz, and which may burn out the bulb, never touch the envelope with bare hands. Just a trace of oil from your skin deposited as a finger-print can have a disastrous result. If the envelope is inadvertently touched, the quartz should be washed clean with methylated spirits, and allowed to dry by evaporation before the bulb is fitted in the headlamp unit.

With age, conventional bulbs darken and this is a sign that the bulb is nearing the end of its life. Since the consequences of a lamp failure are always annoying – and often dangerous – it pays to examine bulbs at regular intervals.

One test is to flick the envelope with a finger. If the filament is sound, this will have no effect. A

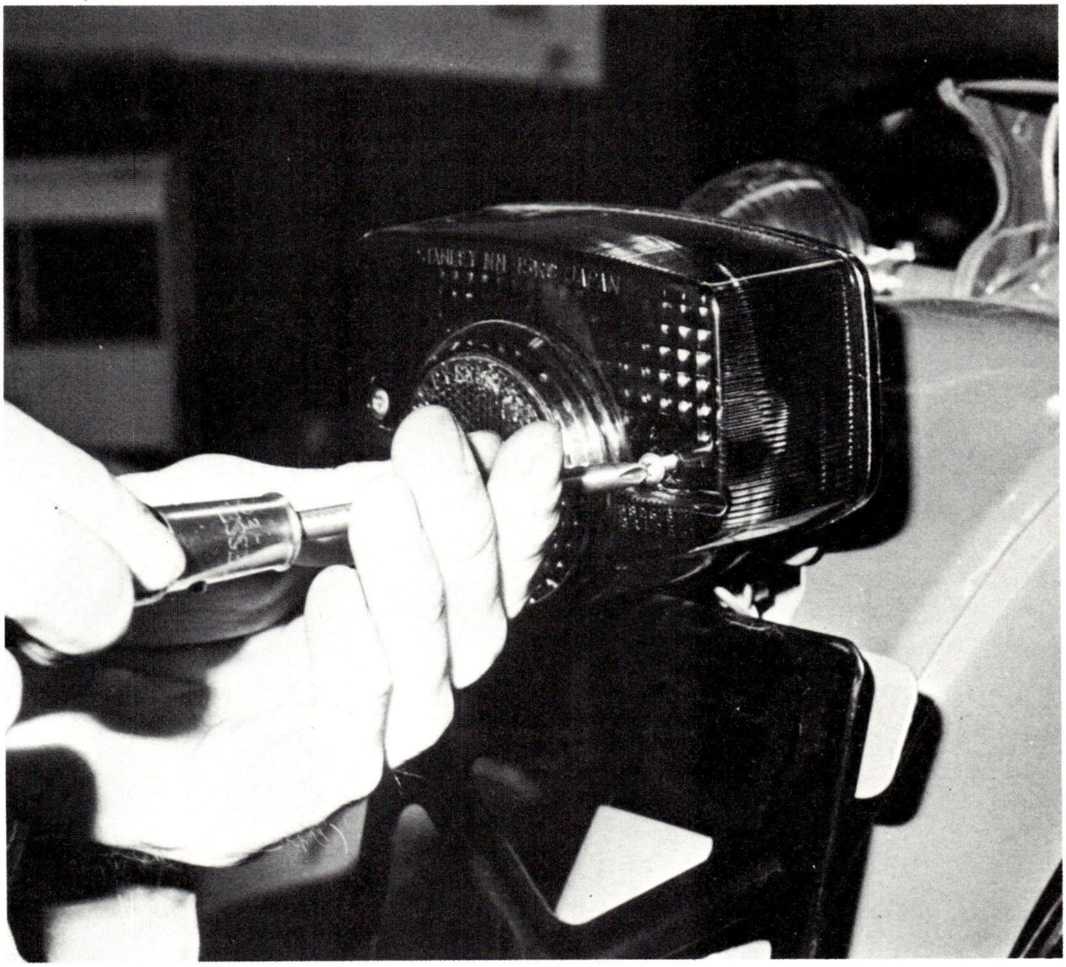

Lens units must have their sealing washers refitted whenever they are removed, or the lamp will fill with water. Take care, also, not to overtighten the screws or the lens may crack

weak filament will fracture, and fall away.

Serviceable bulbs should have their contacts cleaned back to bright metal – oxidisation on the contacts reduces the amount of current that can be fed to the filament – and the lenses of all lamps should be washed periodically with detergent to remove road dirt.

A bulb by itself gives light, but cannot direct it. This job is done by the lamp reflector – a form of parabolic mirror. Like mirrors, reflectors are silvered. Like mirrors, they deteriorate. Unlike mirrors, they cannot usually be cleaned, although where the lens unit is removable it is permissible to wipe the reflector with a very soft and very clean lens cloth, of the type sold by camera shops for use on delicate coated lenses.

Lights that are past their best can often be made to give as-new results by changing the reflector. The deterioration in a reflector's performance is so gradual that a biker may not be aware of this. Four years is about the life it is reasonable to expect, and renewal at this stage of both front and rear reflectors is usually a good investment both in safety and in riding comfort at night.

The Rolling chassis

If the engine/transmission unit is the heart of a motorcycle, then the rolling chassis is its skeleton. Like a skeleton, it is both tough and flexible. Tough, because its main component – the frame – not only carries the weight of the engine, rider, fuel, and ancillaries but maintains the vital alignment of the wheels and absorbs the stresses generated by transmission of the engine power. Flexible, because its suspension system must soak up road irregularities to maintain both directional control and comfort.

Steering

Apart from a few 'specials', every motorcycle built today uses a steering system basically similar to that of the earliest bicycles, built nearly a century ago. The frame carries a short, inclined tube – the steering head. In each end is a bearing. This forms a pivot for the stem of the front forks, which are free to move through an angle of some 60 or 70 degrees from side to side.

The angle at which the head is set – the 'rake' – controls the sensitivity of the bike's steering. The more upright the head, the more sensitive the steering becomes. The reason is that the front wheel actually trails behind its pivot point, like a castor wheel on an .armchair. It is not immediately apparent, because the pivot point is inclined, instead of being vertical, but if a line is drawn straight through the head, and extended to the ground, it will invariably cut the ground-line some inches ahead of a line dropped vertically from the wheel spindle. This distance is the 'trail'. While head angles tend to be fairly constant – about 62° is typical – 'trail' varies noticably between small bikes and superbikes. A 50 cc step-through would have a trail of around 70 mm; a 250 cc sports roadster about 85 mm; and a 1,000 cc superbike something like 120 mm. One reason for these wide variations is, of course, the rolling diameter of the front tyre. The bigger the wheel, the higher off the ground is its spindle – the point from which the perpendicular line of reference originates – and the greater the distance between its point of intersection with the ground and that of the line through the steering head. It follows that if one fitted a wheel of smaller diameter than standard, the effect would be to make the steering more sensitive, since the trail would decrease. Fitting a larger wheel would have the opposite effect.

It is the trail that gives a motorcycle steering its self-centring action. If the wheel is deflected to one side, it automatically tries to recentralise itself. The greater the trail, the stronger the self-centring action becomes.

The layout of the steering also explains why a bike can be cornered merely by banking it in the direction you wish it to go, rather than by turning the handlebars to steer it. As the machine is cranked to one side, the steering head – being rigidly attached to the frame – is moved sideways. The wheel, pivoting behind it, obviously cannot slide sideways without overcoming the grip of the tyre on the road. It therefore turns at an angle to the head. Thanks to the trail, the movement of the wheel is in the correct direction for the turn. Bank left, and the wheel automatically turns left. Bank right, and it turns right. Very satisfying!

Suspension is an aid to steering rather than an essential part of it. Without adequate suspension, a motorcycle would spend quite a lot of its time out of contact with the ground, being launched into

The rear springing on the Yamaha XS750 has five position pre-load adjustment

the air by every bump that could not be absorbed by the flexing of the tyres. Nonetheless, motorcycles *have* been built (and ridden) that had no suspension at all, and rigid rear ends featured on many bikes until well into the 1950s. Part of the reason for this was the difficulty of building a rear suspension system that was light enough for motorcycle use, but strong enough to resist the torsional stresses involved in cornering. It is essential that the rear wheel of a motorcycle should remain absolutely true in the frame. If it moves, it tends to set up an uncontrollable rear-wheel steering effect. And with early rear suspension systems, rear wheels *did* move. . . .

Modern suspension systems are based on the telescopic principle coupled with hydraulic damping. Most front forks are purely telescopic in action. The sliders carrying the wheel move straight up and down the fork stanchion tubes. Rear suspensions, though pivoted so that the rear wheel spindle moves on an arc, use telescopic spring units much like miniature fork legs. Again, these have hydraulic damping.

Dampers are fitted to prevent the suspension oscillating. If a spring is compressed, and then released, its tendency is to continue moving back and forth, in decreasing amounts, until all its stored energy is expended. An undamped suspension spring, therefore, would cause a bike to buck like a bronco for metres after each bump. The damper's job is to keep it under control.

Inside a damper are spring-loaded valves, calibrated holes, and a light oil. A typical twin-tube damper has two valves set in a piston carried on a vertical piston rod, and two more in the pressure chamber formed in the base of the unit. The piston rod is attached to the upper damper mounting on the frame, but not to the lower. The pressure chamber is attached to the lower mounting, but not to the upper. They therefore move relative to each other when the spring unit compresses and rebounds.

On compression, when the bike hits a bump, the oil contained in the inner reservoir in which the piston operates is put under pressure as the damper telescopes. It is the chamber that moves upwards, but the effect is just the same as if the piston were being forced down. As oil is incompressible, there is immediate resistance to movement. If the oil had no escape route, the damper would just lock solid. Instead, the oil is allowed to pass through the piston orifices, and through a non-return valve, into the outer reservoir. As the pressure builds up further, the valves in the foot of the pressure chamber are forced open, and fluid is driven through them too. The resistance offered by the oil absorbs part of the energy of the bump, so controlling movement of the spring. The harder the bump, the greater the damping effect.

On rebound, however, much stiffer damping is required. Although the oil still passes, in the reverse direction, through the calibrated orifices it is a spring-loaded by-pass valve that does the main job. On bump, this was held closed by the pressure of the fluid. On rebound, the power of the damping is controlled by the pressure exerted by the spring on the by-pass valve. The oil that was expelled from the lower chamber on bump is now trapped above the piston, in the top of the pressure chamber. The pressure chamber is trying to move down, but can only do so against the resistance of the trapped oil. The oil cannot escape in quantity until it can build up sufficient pressure to overcome the spring on the valve, and so open the by-pass. The effect is to 'hold back' the rebound.

This is the principle common to twin-tube dampers and to most front telescopic forks, but there is an increasingly-popular alternative – so far as damper units are concerned – in the 'gas shock'. Here, the outer reservoir is discarded, and in its place is a small pocket of inert, bubble-resistant nitrogen gas. With the damper at rest, this sits at the top of the pressure tube. Operate the unit, and the piston and piston rod enter further and further into the tube, so increasing the pressure on the nitrogen. With a twin-tube damper, the resulting aeration would cause air bubbles to form, and since air is compressible these would soon weaken the damping effort. Nitrogen does not aerate: instead, it combines with the fluid to form an emulsion and so maintain the designed damping rate indefinitely, even at high fluid temperatures of 150° C – which is what can be reached during motocross races, for example.

Gas dampers have a further advantage. Conventional units cannot be mounted more than 45° out of the vertical, due to the need to keep the foot valves fully immersed. Therefore, the heaviest part of the damper has to be at the bottom, where it contributes considerably to the unsprung weight of the rear suspension. Gas shocks, however, can be mounted inverted, so that the lightest parts are at the bottom, with consequent benefit to the handling.

Nitrogen-filled dampers should not be confused with pneumatic suspension systems. In the gas shock, the nitrogen is used as part of the damping system, and the actual springing is still by means of coil springs. Pneumatic units dispense with springs completely, using instead air that is compressed by the action of a piston, just like the operation of the piston in the cylinder of the engine. Though offering some advantages in flexibility in the rate of the springing, air suspension has the disadvantage of needing the units on both sides of the spindle to be coupled to ensure balance: and the system does rely heavily on its seals.

Most machines built today have

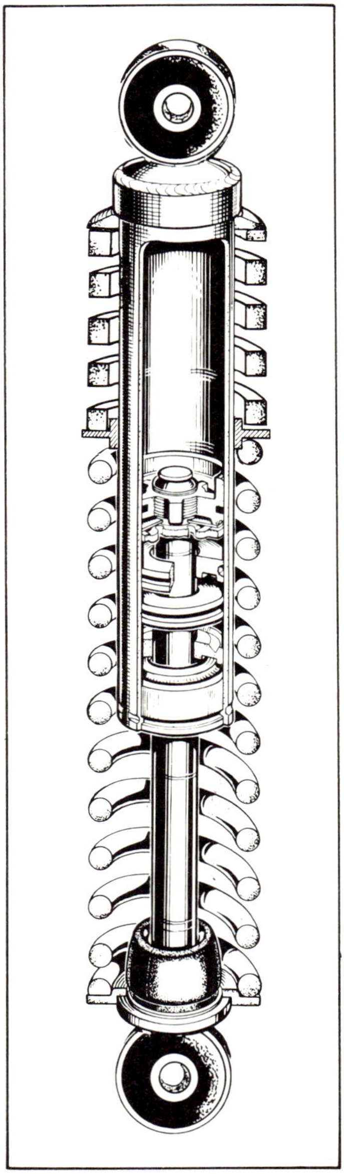

The latest idea in dampers – the Gas Shock, pioneered by the Girling company. The relatively heavy chamber carrying the damper fluid is mounted uppermost, so that it becomes part of the sprung weight. The light piston rod moves with the suspension, instead of being static as on earlier designs. The chamber also contains inert nitrogen gas, to prevent aeration and give uniform damping at high fluid temperatures. The spring/damper unit shown here also uses Girling's double-spring principle to give a variable rate. The heavy minor spring is the square-sectioned one at the top. It is separated from the lighter round-section major spring by a sliding nylon collar.

coil springs for both front and rear. Previously, both leaf springs and rubber springs were used. Sometimes the springs are multi-rate, with windings of different strength at top and bottom. The idea is to give sensitivity to small bumps, with progressive stiffening as fork movement increases. An alternative is the Girling system in which a major spring and a minor spring are combined to get the advantages of both.

It works by using the springs 'in series', so that their characteristic rates combine to give a surprisingly wide range of capabilities. The 'rate' of a spring is the amount of pressure required to compress it by one inch. The greater the pressure, the higher the rate and the stiffer the spring.

A typical combination in a Girling damper would be a major spring of 145 lb in, with a minor spring of 180 lb in mounted above it. This gives an initial spring rate of just over 80 lb in – a seemingly impossible result until you look at the mathematics involved.

Assume that a load of 180 lb is applied to the unit. That compresses the minor spring by one inch. Since the minor spring and major spring rest on each other, the major spring also compresses. Its total movement can be calculated by dividing the minor spring rate by the major spring rate – in this case, $180 \div 145 = 1{\cdot}24$ in. Add the one inch movement of the minor spring, and total movement is 2·24 in. The initial spring rate can be calculated by dividing the minor spring rate by the total movement – in this example, $180 \div 2{\cdot}24 = 80{\cdot}36$ lb in.

So, the use of two relatively heavy springs actually provides the flexibility wanted for small road irregularities; and when it comes to a major bump the effect is to compress the short minor spring to the point where it closes up completely and becomes solid, leaving the long major spring to operate at its own designed heavy rating.

Chassis care

It goes without saying that the rolling chassis needs careful maintenance, just like the more obviously mechanical parts of the bike, if the steering, suspension, and braking are to be kept at designed standard.

The first essential is that the steering head itself should be in good order. Two types of head bearing are in current use – ball races, and taper-roller races.

Ball races are the familiar cycle-type bearings, in which uncaged bearing balls operate in upper and lower tracks. The bottom head bearing has a lower track mounted on the bottom front fork bridge and an upper track set into the bottom of the head tube. The upper head bearing has its lower track sunk into the top of the head tube, and its upper track formed into the underside of a cap which screws on to the fork stem. This is the steering head adjustment: screwing down the upper race tightens the bearings; unscrewing it loosens them.

With taper-roller bearings the general layout is similar. In each case, the outer track of the bearing is an interference fit in the steering head, and the inner races – comprising the caged rollers and the inner track – are fitted over the stem. A screwed cap bears on the upper inner race, forcing it into closer engagement with the track when it is screwed down.

Steering head adjustment

A loose steering head bearing causes the steering to wander, since the forks become free to move slightly from side to side, and backwards and forwards, as well as pivoting. Under braking, the bike can also tend to lurch, and the wheel may tend to chop away down the camber. Tight head bearings, on the other hand, make the bike very hard to steer, since the self-centring action is impaired. The machine therefore tends to snake along the road.

Rectification of either fault is easy, so long as the head bearings themselves have not been damaged. Where looseness is the fault, bearing damage is unlikely. Since tight bearings have been clamped down beyond their normal limit, this can cause a series of faults. With ball races, overtightening can cause one or more of the following faults: distorted bearing balls; cracked bearing balls; indented races; break-up of the case hardening on the tracks; pitting of the tracks and/or balls; hairline cracks in the balls or races.

With taper-roller bearings, which have in effect line contact between each roller and the tracks, over-tightening can have the disastrous result of indenting the contact faces, so turning the race almost into a form of ratchet.

It is important, therefore, that the steering head adjustment should be made with the greatest of care and with delicate use of the tools involved – usually, a C-spanner to turn the adjuster cap, and an open-ended spanner large enough to fit any locking nut that is used.

Start by blocking up the machine securely, under the crankcase, so that the front wheel is completely clear of the ground. Head bearings *cannot* be adjusted while there is weight on the wheel.

Next, it is often necessary to remove the front fork upper bridge to gain access to the screwed adjuster cap. On some bikes, this is an irksome job, entailing removal of the speedo and tachometer, and sometimes of the complete handlebar/light unit assembly as well. Before doing so, therefore, it is just as well to check that the bearings do in fact need adjustment! It is easily done. First, set the forks centrally and then gently tap one side of the bars. The forks should swing to the opposite side under their own weight. Repeat the test on the other side, bearing in mind that the wiring harness and control cables may tend to damp out movement a little. If the forks swing freely almost as far as the steering stops there is no question of their being over-tightened. One obvious point may be overlooked, however – if a steering damper is fitted it should be freed off (if of the friction type) or disconnected (if hydraulic) before this test is made.

To check for loose bearings, grasp the wheel at the spindle and place your thumb across the gap between the lower bridge and the steering head. Try pressing the spindle backwards and then pulling it forwards. You should feel no movement on your thumb. If you do, it shows that the forks can move longitudinally, and that the bearings are loose.

To adjust either type of bearing, slacken off the locknut on the stem, and either release the screwed cap slightly to free off the bearings, or screw it down to reduce play. Where possible, always screw down with your fingers rather than a spanner – your touch is more sensitive that way.

While adjusting the bearings, keep checking the free side-to-side movement of the forks. If this is becoming impaired, slacken off slightly. When you reach a setting that gives free movement from lock to lock, with no perceptible longitudinal play of the forks, the adjustment is spot on. Fit the requisite spanner to the cap, and hold it steady while you tighten the locknut. Any attempt to lock the nut without holding the screw cap will almost certainly upset the adjustment you have been careful to find. To be on the safe side, recheck the setting after it has been locked, but before refitting the bridge, etc.

Lubricating head bearings

Save for the handful of machines that still have grease nipples for the bearings, lubrication is a job to be done when the forks are removed, since there is no other means of access to the lower bearing. Providing the races have been properly packed with grease on assembly, there should normally be no need for further attention, since the bearings are totally enclosed and are not subjected to heat.

Split ball races are assembled with grease. The tracks fixed in the steering head are lined with grease, and so are the tracks fitted to the front fork bridge and the adjuster cap. The bearing balls are then fitted into their 'nest' of grease in each of the upwards-facing tracks, and the forks are offered up and the bearings adjusted.

With taper-roller bearings, the tracks are lightly greased, and grease is packed into each of the inner races and worked into the roller cages. The assembly is then completed.

Renewing head bearings

While the exact methods vary from bike to bike, the general procedure for renewing head bearings is the same. Remove the wheel. Then the top bridge must be lifted. It is usually easiest to do this without disconnecting the wiring harnesses or all the control cables, simply by freeing the stem nut – and sometimes the fork leg bolts – and swinging the complete assembly clear of the forks. Where this is done, wrap rags round the

Typical steering head layout, using taper-roller bearings. The bearing is set into the head, under a dust cap. It is locked and adjusted by means of a castellated ring nut

The bottom bearing is carried on the lower yoke, and has no individual means of adjustment

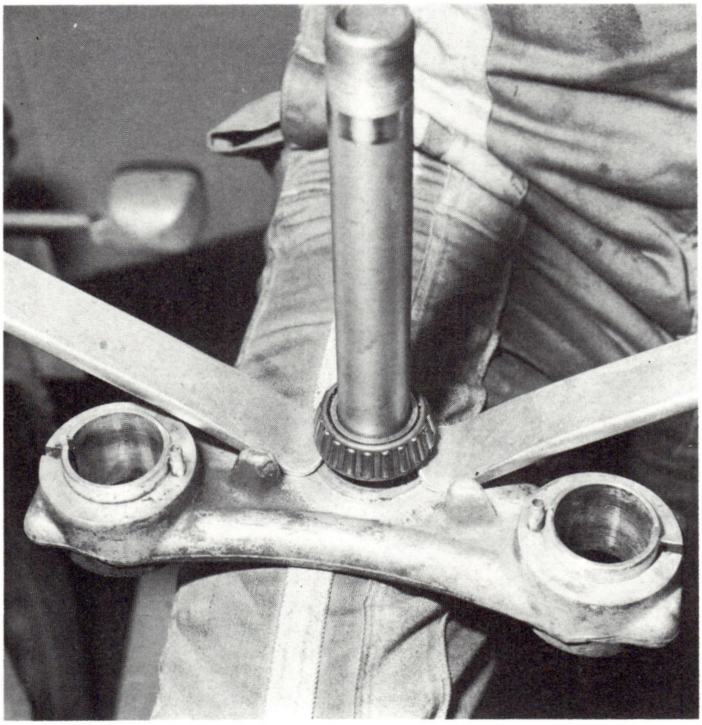

Inner races are a press fit, and can be removed with the help of tyre levers

The outer tracks can be driven out by means of a drift inserted from below, providing there is sufficient protuberance for the drift to engage. Otherwise, a special puller such as this is needed

Before refitting, the roller races must be packed with grease. This lubrication will last for upwards of 20,000 miles

With ball-type races, the lubricating grease is used to locate the balls on the track during assembly

bars to act as padding, and use aero-elastic to hold them clear of the forks while the work proceeds.

Support the forks with a block of wood, and undo the locknut and adjuster. Then, supporting the forks by hand, let them drop slowly out of the head.

A few bikes, such as the BMW range, demand a more complicated procedure. Here, the fork legs themselves have to be removed individually, before the yoke/stem assembly is detached. While fork leg removal is simple – freeing off the pinch bolts at the upper bridge and the yoke unclamps them – it does also mean that the mudguard has to be detached separately.

Disc brakes present a problem, too. With drum brakes, it is enough to unhook the cable and free the torque arm, when the brake simply comes away with the wheel. Hydraulically-operated discs are a different proposition, and the choice is between leaving the brake caliper attached to the fork, and freeing the hose; or detaching the caliper and keeping the hose intact. In the former case, the brakes will have to be bled on reassembly. In the latter, great care must be taken not to let the calipers hang on the hoses, and so run the risk of stressing the pipework.

With the forks off, the bearings can be removed and new races fitted. To detach the tracks from the head, the usual method is to insert a long drift from the opposite end of the head tube, and butt it against the edge of the race. A sharp hammer blow should dislodge it, and it can then be tapped out. Some bikes, though, have very close-fitting races that demand the use of an expanding extractor – a rather rare tool, unfortunately, although a tool-hire shop may have one. Brute-force methods such as using a hammer and cold chisel to break up the old race are not recommended. There is not only the danger of damage to a vital part of the bike – important though that is – but splinters of hardened metal are likely to fly out as the race is cut, and they can be as damaging as buckshot to unprotected hands, faces, and eyes.

Happily, most races come away easily, and those on the steering stem can be levered off with a pair of stout tyre levers. Fitting new tracks entails nothing more complicated than driving each home with a hammer and a block of wood. With taper rollers, where the inner race goes on the stem, press it on as far as it will go, and then place a suitably-sized box spanner over the stem and use it to tap the bearing fully home. Short taps around the race with a soft-metal drift will do the trick as well.

Before assembly, lubricate the bearings with grease, and then rebuild and adjust the forks.

Swinging fork pivot bearing

The majority of current motorcycles have plain, non-adjustable bearings for the rear swinging fork pivot. The few exceptions – usually shaft-drive machines – employ either taper-roller bearings similar to those in the steering head, or some other form of taper adjustment.

A non-adjustable bearing that has worn can cause the bike to weave, since the rear fork is then free to move slightly from side to side. Renewal is the only proper course, and the general procedure is as follows:

With the bike on its stand, detach the rear wheel. With disc-braked models, remove the caliper and tie it to the subframe, out of harm's way. Then remove the bolts from the lower ends of the rear spring units, and swing them away from the fork. Take off any other encumbrances – the chainguard, for example – and then undo the nut on the swinging fork pivot spindle. Tap out the spindle, using a soft-metal drift, if it is too tight a fit to be withdrawn by hand.

The swinging fork can now be lifted from the bike for attention to the bearings. The exact design details differ – for example, some makers fit dust seals and others do not. These are normally no more than a cap, containing an 'O' ring seal and perhaps a thrust washer. The bearing itself is generally either a bush inserted into each end of the swinging fork, with a central spacer interposed; a long bush through the fork; or two short bushes in a cutaway pivot, with a frame member separating them.

Drive out the old bushes, and then wash the pivot assembly with petrol or paraffin, and allow it to dry before inserting the new parts. Grease the spacer, where fitted, and push it into the pivot. Grease one of the replacement bushes, then insert and drive it home, using a hammer and a block of softwood. Fit the other bush in a similar manner. Grease the pivot spindle, fit any dust seals – new 'O'-rings should always be used – and rebuild the suspension.

Wheel bearings

Front and rear wheel bearings are usually of the non-adjustable, ball-race type. Where bearings show signs of wear, they must be replaced, because worn bearings can seriously affect handling.

The wheel bearing arrangement is similar to the rear fork pivot bearing, except that ball bearings are used instead of plain bearings. In both wheels, the bearings operate on a spindle, and are an interference fit in their housings with a central spacer between them. Invariably, a grease seal is fitted outside each bearing to prevent any leakage of lubricant. In some drum-brake systems, one seal is located in the brake backplate rather than in the hub.

To renew bearings, first remove the wheel, then ease the oil seal from the hub – usually, it can be 'winkled' out with a screwdriver; but be careful not to damage it. Each bearing can then be driven out of its housing using a hammer and a drift inserted from the opposite side and butted against the inner face of the bearing.

When fitting new bearings, first line the inside of the hub with a layer of grease, up to a quarter of an inch thick. Insert the greased spacer, and pack each bearing with grease. Offer up and drive in one bearing; check that the spacer is properly seated; then drive in the other bearing. Refit the oil seals – purists renew them – and wipe away any grease that has been squeezed out during assembly.

Rims and spokes

Steering faults can sometimes be traced to distorted wheel rims or loose or broken spokes. With conventional wire-wheel construction, the machine in effect 'hangs' from the spokes that are uppermost as the wheel revolves, and if these are loose the rim can squirm under power, so inducing weave.

The easiest check for spoke tension is to turn the wheel, pressing each pair of spokes together at the point at which they cross. No movement should be felt. Do not rely on the method – sometimes advocated by folk who should know better – of tapping the spoke with a screwdriver and judging its tension by the sound. You are *not* Yehudi Menuhin!

The odd loose spoke can be tightened, using – preferably – a spoke key. This slides over the nipple, and has a built-in tommy bar to allow it to be turned. In an emergency, a small adjustable spanner can be used but remember that space around the nipples is limited.

Turning a spoke nipple – in effect, simply an elongated nut – screws the nipple up the spoke, which means that as the nipple is turned the end of the spoke begins to stand proud of the wheel rim. One turn of the nipple will not make this protrusion excessive. However, if a nipple needs more than a single turn, then the wheel must be detached; the tyre and tube must be removed; the rim tape must be lifted out; and when the spoke has been tensioned, the part standing proud must be ground away. This is a safety precaution to prevent any possibility of the spoke jabbing into the tube and causing a blow-out, with disastrous results.

Spoke tension controls the truth of the wheel, and although one or two loose spokes will not usually cause excessive rim run-out, any significant number of slack or broken ones almost certainly will.

A rough check for wheel truth is to clamp a large nail to the bike with a worm-drive clip so that the nail point just touches the side of the rim. By gently turning the wheel observe whether the rim just skims the nail all the way round indicating that the wheel is running true. Any gaps showing between the nail and parts of the rim mean the wheel is out of truth. Truing a rim is a job for a wheel-builder. You can do a passable emergency job yourself, drawing the rim in by tightening some spokes and loosening others, but to be accurate takes a craftsman's touch.

Again, a spoke *can* be renewed without removing the wheel. The damaged spoke is simply unscrewed from the nipple. Then the tyre is deflated sufficiently for the nipple to be pressed down almost flush with the rim, and the new spoke is threaded into place. Engage it with the nipple; then tighten the nipple to tension the spoke. Providing the new spoke has been filed to ensure that it is the same length exactly as the one that broke, this method is an acceptable stop-gap. But, again, the counsel of perfection is to do the job with a bare wheel, and to grind down the spoke afterwards. It is time-consuming: but not as much as repairing the after-effects of a tyre blow-out at speed would be.

Wheel balancing

Ideally, any road wheel should be in perfect balance. In practice, parts of the wheel are heavier than others – the tyre valve, for example, makes for an asymmetric load – and at speed the heavier section of the wheel tends to fly outwards and set up oscillation in the springing. Balance that is wrong laterally can shake the steering.

The answer is wheel balancing. Nowadays, this is normally done at the factory, when the wheel is built. Lead weights are added, until the wheel is balanced. Providing the tyres are then properly fitted when they are renewed, the wheel balance should remain correct indefinitely.

Balance weights can, however, become lost. If they are, the best procedure is to have the wheel professionally re-balanced, since it is then done on a proper rig, and perhaps with the aid of dynamic balancing machines. These take the guesswork out of the operation.

To balance a wheel at home, it helps to make up a rig in which the wheel can be mounted, but it can be done on the bike providing the brake caliper or brake plate (drum brakes) is removed so there is no drag; and any other components that could cause drag – eg, the rear chain or the speedo drive – are first disconnected. The bike is then raised until the wheel is free to spin.

Ideally, use lead balancing weights made for the job. Alternatively, lead 'tape' (try your local builder's merchant!) wound round a spoke and properly secured will do the trick.

Spin the wheel, let it run to rest and note where it stops. Mark the lowest point at which the wheel comes to rest with chalk or a grease pencil; then spin it again. You will probably find that one particular section of the wheel always swings back to end up at the bottom. That is the heaviest section of the wheel, and to balance it you need to weight that part of the wheel exactly opposite. Fit your lightest balance weight, or a turn of lead tape, and try again. If the original heavier section still ends up at the bottom, you need more weight opposite, so use the next-heaviest weight you have, or wind on a bit more tape. Eventually, you will reach the point at which no one part of the wheel consistently finishes up lowermost, and your wheel is then in balance.

Tyres

Tyre fitting also has an effect on handling. If the tyre does not sit concentrically on the rim, it has an effect similar to that of an off-balance wheel. The wheel, in effect, becomes egg-shaped. Similarly, a tyre that is fitted with a twist in its carcass gives the same shake to the steering that would be experienced with lateral imbalance.

Tyres normally have a fitting line moulded round the casing.

This line must be parallel to the rim, on both sides of the tyre. Also, tyres are pre-balanced at the factory, and the section that is to be adjacent to the tyre valve is marked with a spot of paint. Get this wrong, and your wheel balance is automatically disturbed. Lastly, some tyres have a direction of rotation arrow moulded to the tyre wall. This indicates which way round the tyre should go for optimum tread wear: but the direction of rotation can differ from front wheel to back. When fitting a tyre, therefore, be certain that the direction of rotation is correct for the particular application you are using.

Tyre removal

Do not try removing a motorcycle cover with the wheel still in the bike – it just cannot be done that way. Instead, take off the wheel so that you can lay it flat on the ground. Then let out all remaining air – in the case of a puncture, the tyre is rarely absolutely flat – by using the core removal tool on the end of the valve cap to detach the entire valve core. Do not lose it!

Step on the cover all the way round, to expel the last of the air and to break the bead. Take off the valve locknut. With the bead broken, carry on removing the cover if you are doing a roadside repair. In the workshop, ease the job for yourself by brushing tyre lubricant round the joint between rim and bead. Washing-up liquid will do the trick.

Start removal adjacent to the valve, inserting two tyre levers about 6 in apart. Press on them, to lift that section of the bead over the rim. Now take out one lever, and insert it 3 in further on. Press on it, to lift a further 3 in of bead. Repeat the operation with the other lever, and then go back to the first, and carry on in this way until the cover is half off.

Now place one hand flat on the spokes to give yourself a fulcrum and use the other to ease the rest of the cover clear.

Start directly opposite the valve, and lift out the tube. When you get to the valve, twist the bead open with one hand while the other jabs smartly down on to the top of the valve to press it through its hole. With the tube removed, use the levers to start the other beading over the rim. Here, you need only about a foot of cover clear of the wheel, and the rest will slide out easily.

If the cover is to be refitted, clean it out thoroughly to get rid of any trapped grit. While it is off, check it for penetration by nails, glass or stones, and remove any trapped stones from the treads.

Puncture repairs

It is useless trying to stick a patch to a tube that has not been 'keyed'. The patch will not seat properly – or, worse, it will seem to take and then lift off again to re-open the puncture.

The first step in repairing a tube is to locate the hole, either by inflating the tube and immersing it in water; or by inflating it and locating the puncture by ear and eye. When the puncture is found, dry the tube in that area, and set to work with some coarse emery cloth to remove the silicon bloom from the surface. This is the silver dust that gets all over your hands whenever you handle a tube, and it is also the stuff that prevents the patch from sticking.

With your emery cloth, clean an area slightly larger than the patch you plan to fit. Then, using a *clean* finger, smear vulcanising fluid all over the area where the patch is to go. Do not touch it again once you have applied it: except just on the outer edge to check that it is tacky. When the

The following illustrations show how to repair a puncture.
First find the hole! A puncture such as this can be located by inspection, or the hiss of air escaping when the tube is inflated. Slow punctures demand immersion in a bowl of water – and watch for the bubbles. If the seam is split, or the puncture is around the base of the valve, a new tube will be needed

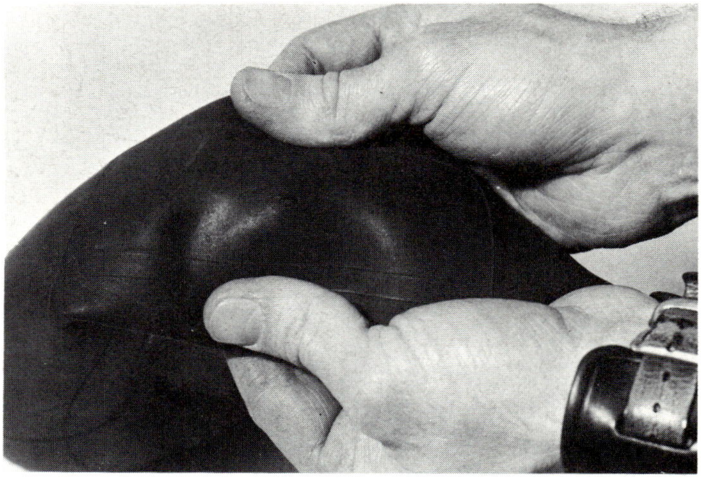

Patches will not adhere to dirt or grease: and your finger-marks are greasy. So, start by cleaning the area round the puncture. Trichloroethylene is the best solvent, but petrol will do. Do *not* use petroil from a two-stroke's tank After cleaning the tube, use sandpaper to roughen up the area where the patch is to go, plus a little extra round it

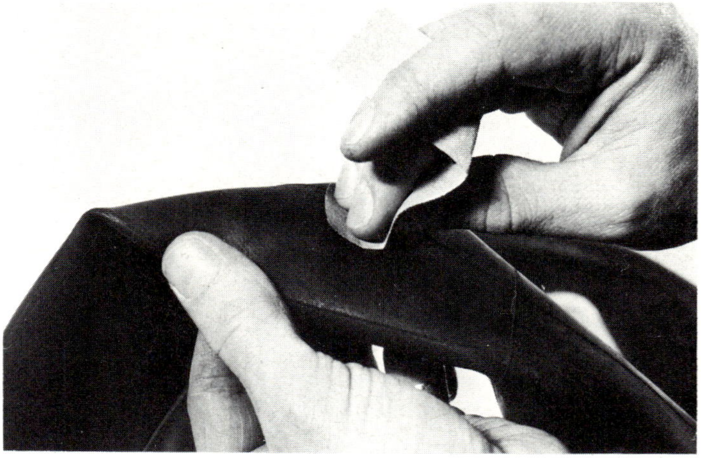

Where the rubber has split, rather than just punctured, press the sides of the split together and bevel off the edges with sandpaper. This will bond the patch to the edges, giving better adhesion and reducing the risk of the split spreading under the patch

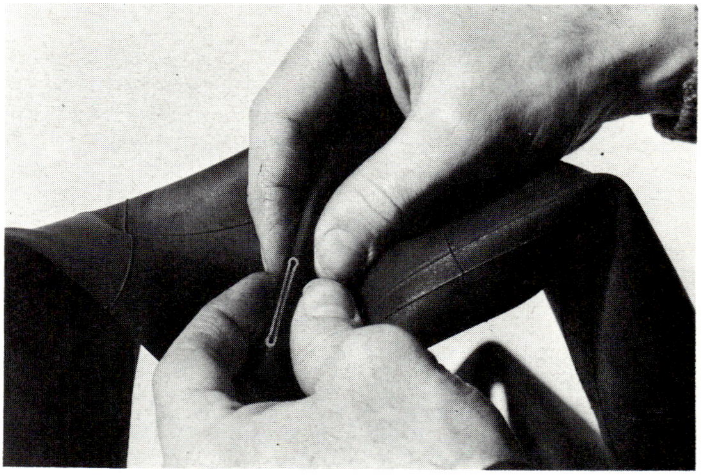

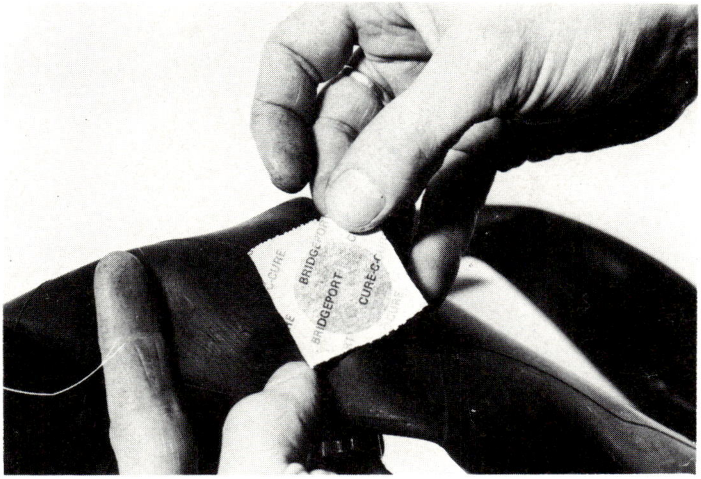

Offer up a patch to check for size. For holes, the patch must be at least three times the area of the puncture. For splits, it must be no less than 1½ times as long

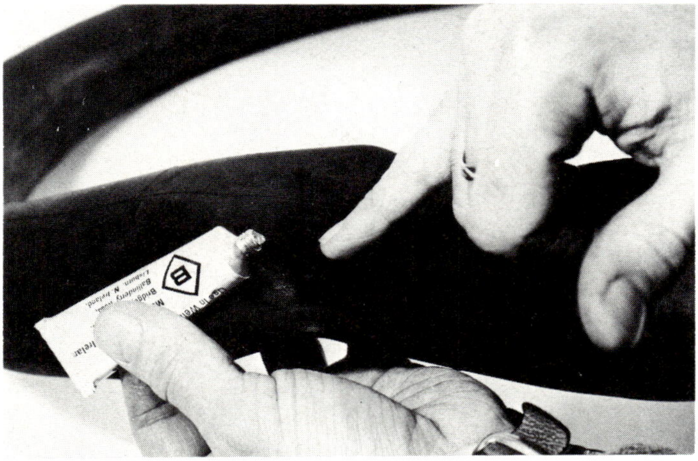

With a clean finger, prime the roughened area with rubber solution. Give it a minute or so to dry. Then check the very edge of the primed area with your finger. It should feel tacky. If so, apply a second thin layer of solution

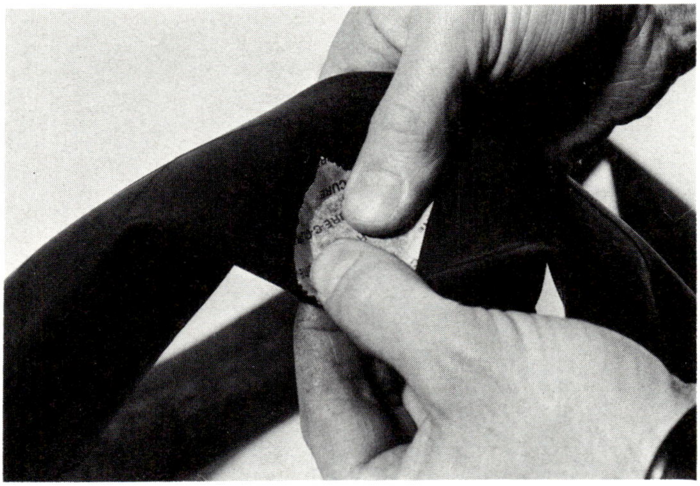

Let the second coating go tacky. Then peel the metal foil from the patch, and press the centre of the patch on to the hole. Press the rest down firmly with your fingers, working outwards all the time

Lastly, pinch the patch until the backing paper cracks. Then peel off the paper, again working from the centre outwards. Make sure that in doing so you do not lift the feathered edges of the patch. If there is any excess rubber solution, dust it with French Chalk: but do not overdo it, or the chalk may harden and chafe the tube later on

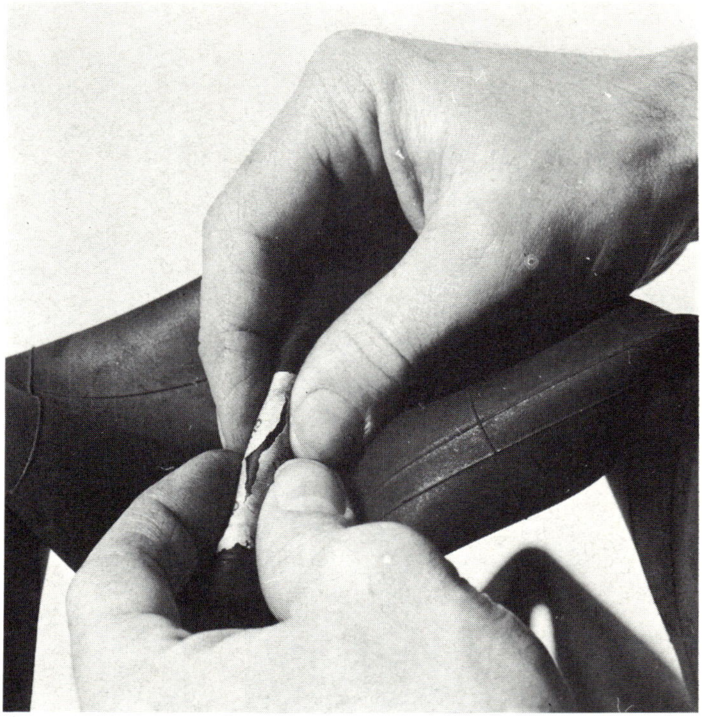

Getting the tyre off is easy: getting it back on without damaging the tube takes know-how. And the first trick of the trade is to lubricate the tyre beads thoroughly, using either a tyre lubricant or ordinary washing-up liquid

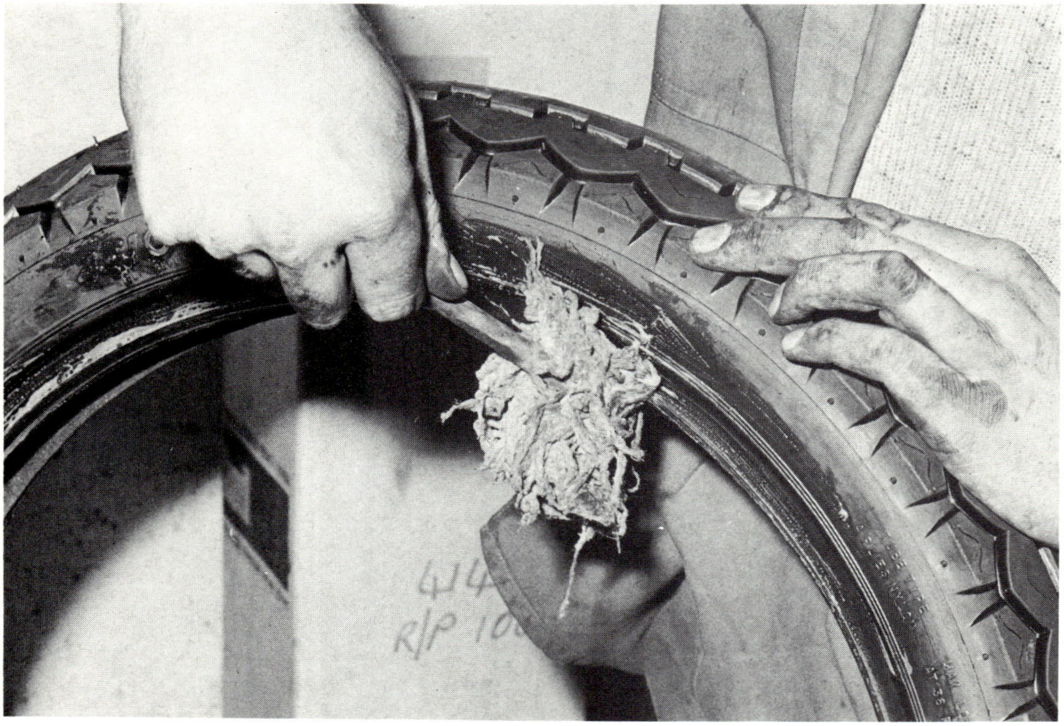

Lay the wheel flat, and offer up the cover. Check whether it has an arrow indicating the direction of rotation. If so, make sure it is pointing the right way. Then press the well-lubricated bead over the rim

Some tyres are marked for balance as well. These three dots indicate the area that has to go next to the valve. Adjust the position of the cover so they line up accurately with the valve orifice

You cannot fit a tube like this! If it is flat, it will likely get trapped. So, inflate it just a little – in this photograph, the tube underneath shows how much – before you try to insert it

Use your knee to press the cover down while you thread the valve through its hole. Then fit the valve securing nut, tightening it up by only a few threads. Any security bolts should already have been installed, and their nuts also run on similarly

Press the tube into the tyre, and even it up all round. Make sure it has gone over the security bolt flanges (where fitted), and apply a little more lubricant all round between the rim and the tyre bead

Turn the wheel so the valve is away from you, and then start pressing the cover over the rim with both hands

Work a few inches at a time in each direction until you have left just a length of bead centred on the tyre valve. Press the security bolts right in as you pass them

Now apply some more lubricant to the remaining bead, and push the valve fully in. This ensures the tube will not be trapped. The last few inches of bead should now twist easily over the rim

solution is tacky, peel the backing from the patch, and place it squarely over the prepared surface. Press it down in the middle first, and then work outwards from the centre until it is fully adhered to the tube. Finish off with just a light dusting of French chalk.

Tyre fitting

Wipe the lower bead of the cover with tyre lubricant, and offer it up to the wheel. Press the lower bead over the wheel rim all the way round. Given luck, it will slip on easily. Otherwise, hold the far end of the bead into contact with the rim, insert a lever dead opposite, and ease the rest home.

Fit the valve core – or, if it is a new tube, check that the core is tight. Then inflate the tube just sufficiently for it to take up its shape and insert into the cover.

After making sure the tube is tucked in, press the lower bead down into the well of the rim, all the way round. Lubricate the upper bead, and begin easing it over the rim, starting at a point diametrically opposite to the valve. As with removal, work alternately from side to side, easing 3 in of bead at a time over the rim. You will end up with a section of cover that seems skin-tight right across the wheel.

At this point, refit the valve locknut, but only screw it down until it is level with the top of the valve. Now push the valve right down, until the nut contacts the face of the rim, and insert a lever 6 in from the valve. Using one hand to keep the bead pushed down into the well while the other hand operates the lever, ease the bead over the rim until you reach the last 9 to 12 in of bead. Then insert a lever at each end and operate them simultaneously to slide the last section over the rim. After the tyre is fitted, pull down on the valve and tighten up the locknut far enough for the pump to be coupled up.

Pump up the tyre to 45 psi – a pressure high enough to blow the beads into their correct positions in the rim – and check the moulded centring line. If it's out of true, deflate the tube, unscrew the locknut to the end of the valve stem, again press the valve in as far as the nut allows, and brush more lubricant round the bead. Re-inflating to 45 psi should then correctly position the centring line. After setting the correct pressure, tighten down the locknut and refit the valve cap, which forms the secondary seal. Lastly, where a security bolt is fitted, make sure that it is tightened, and then refit the wheel.

Front forks

At the present time, all designers favour front fork systems that are either telescopic in action, or rely on one of several variations on the swinging-link theme.

Link-type front forks can be regarded as miniature versions of a rear suspension system, using separate spring/damper units, and the same overhaul techniques should be applied when servicing them.

Telescopic forks also follow a fairly general design pattern. Each fork leg is an entity, comprising a stanchion; a spring or springs; a slider carrying the wheel spindle; and in-built hydraulic damping. Each leg is clamped into the fork yoke and steadied by the fork bridge. In some instances the fork-leg bolts lock the top of the leg to the bridge: in others they are simply plugs. Sometimes they form the upper spring anchorage: but they may also themselves contain a screwed plug for topping up the fork oil.

Most front suspension troubles can be traced either to a poor

Check that the tube is not trapped; screw up the valve and security bolt fastenings (where fitted); and inflate the tyre. If you used enough lubricant the bead lines will lie parallel to the rim. If not, blow the tyre up hard – about 45 psi – and then reduce the pressure to the recommended setting

damping action, or to wear in the slider bushes. The cure for the first-named fault is invariably to use a different grade of oil. The normal fork oil is of high viscosity – automatic transmission fluid; or a 10W/30 engine oil. For heavier duties, it often pays to substitute the thicker 20W/50 engine oil, whose damping characteristics appear to be more suited to West European motorcycling conditions.

Fork stripping

The simplest way to dismantle a fork is to work on one leg at a time. There is rarely any need to disturb the steering-head bearings, but all obstructions, such as the mudguard, brakes, etc., are removed before the fork leg clamps are undone. The leg can then be pulled out of the yoke. In some instances, where the headlamp is carried on a fork shroud surrounding the leg, this can be left undisturbed, securely trapped between the yoke and the bridge.

Once removed, the leg should be drained of oil. A drain screw is often located on the side of the slider, otherwise, the fork cap bolt should be removed and the oil poured out. With Ceriani-type forks, the spring is also released by removal of the cap bolt (see lower illustration on page 158).

A push-on dust seal is normally fitted over the top of the slider. Move this out of the way, when the collar can be unscrewed from the slider. Before unscrewing the collar with either a strap wrench or chain wrench, protect it by wrapping with heavy rag, or with a piece of rubber cut from a discarded inner tube. Underneath, there is usually an O-ring and the fork bush, which can be slid out of position. These bushes and their

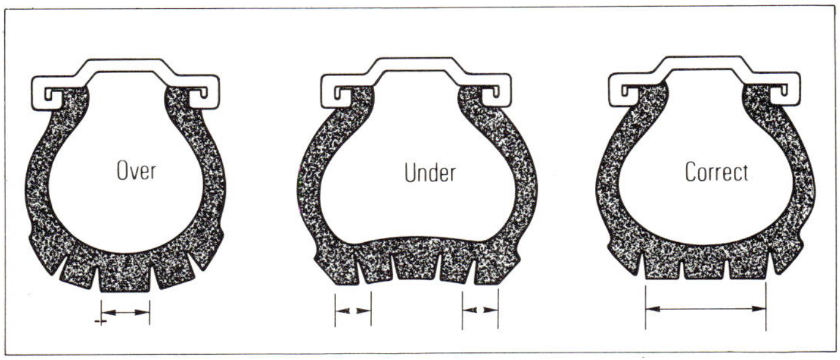

Showing why correct inflation pressure is essential. Over-inflating the tyre means that the area in contact with the road is confined to the centre of the tread. This then wears out fast. With an under-inflated tyre, the opposite happens. The centre of the tread tends to bow up from the road, and wear is then concentrated on two small areas to each side. Only correct inflation spreads the load – and therefore the wear – evenly over the entire contact 'footprint'

Stripping Telescopic Forks
1. To strip telescopic forks, the easiest way is to remove the legs from the yokes. On most designs, the legs can be pulled out after loosening the clamping bolts, leaving the upper shrouds in place.

The individual legs can then be checked for wear by pressing the stanchion tube and slider in opposite directions. Any movement means worn bushes.
2. Remove the road spring by detaching the plug bolt at the top of the fork. Some types of fork have twin springs: others one spring wound so that it gives different rates of compression. Always check the way the spring is placed, so that it can be refitted properly.
3. Just how the slider is held depends upon the individual design, although most forks are similar in construction. On this Suzuki type, there is a socket-headed screw set vertically in the end of the slider. Undo it, and the slider is free.

associated oil seals are the only parts of the fork normally prone to wear.

A variant is used on some Honda and Suzuki models, where the lower slider is secured by a socket bolt or an Allen screw inserted vertically upwards through the spindle yoke. Remove the fork leg and drain the oil as before. Then remove the socket bolt, which often requires the use of a special spanner. With the bolt out, the slider can be pulled away from the stanchion. On forks of this design, the damper unit and spring may remain with the stanchion.

The vulnerable part on this fork is the oil seal, which is set into the upper part of the slider. To renew the seal, use circlip pliers to remove the oil seal's circlip, and then winkle out the oil seal. The new seal must be accurately driven home – lubricate it with oil before offering it up – and the circlip firmly reseated.

Swinging-link forks

Apart from replacement of the spring/damper units, the only servicing normally required on forks of this type is to renew the pivot bearings. These are plain bushes, in which runs a short pin which is often through-drilled for lubrication, and equipped with a grease nipple.

Rear spring/damper units

Most current spring/damper units are sealed, and no work is possible on them apart from removing the springs for fitting to a new unit. The method of fixing is by collet. To remove the spring, it must be compressed – preferably with a spring compressor. It is possible, however, to do the job in a vice, providing you have first made up three suitably-sized spring hooks which will keep the springs compressed when inserted. The top collet can then be freed, the spring

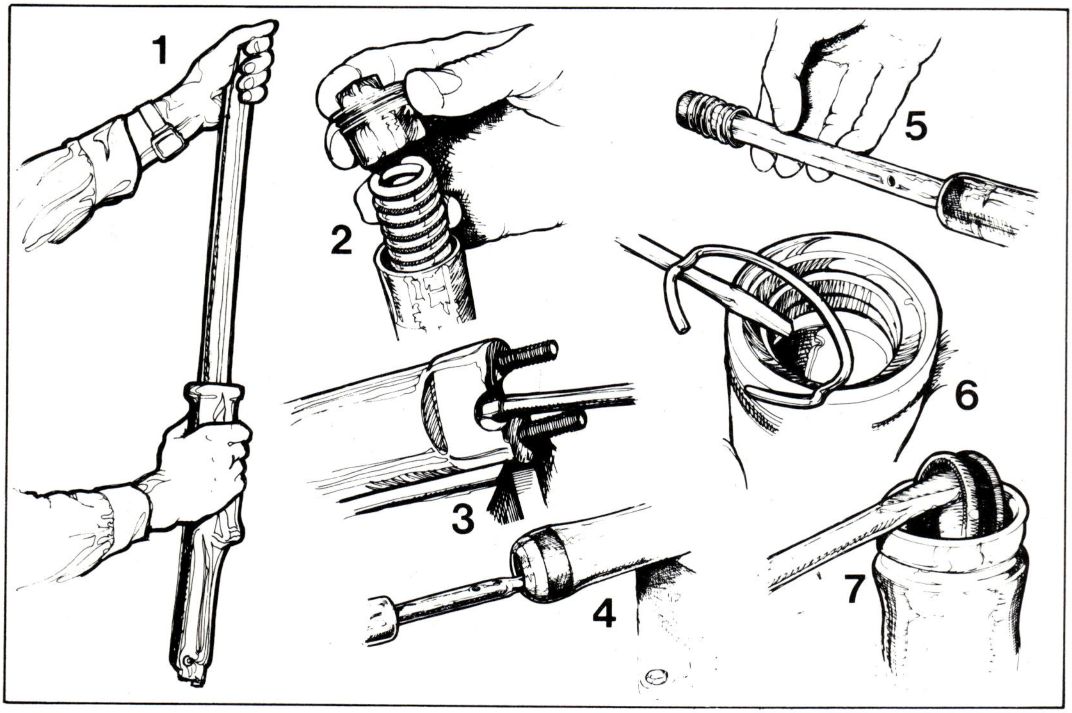

gently released, and fitted to the new damper unit.

One damper manufacturer – Koni – incorporate an adjustment for the damping. Designed to compensate for wear in the system, it entails removing the spring and bump rubber. With the damper's lower eye locked in a vice, the unit is fully compressed and the piston rod is turned to engage in an internal adjusting nut. Revolving it up to a maximum of two and a quarter turns blanks off several internal orifices and stiffens up the internal by-pass valve spring to give a heavier damping action.

4. The stanchion tube simply pulls away from the slider.
5. On the end of the stanchion is the damper piston. This assembly never normally gives trouble providing the fork oil is changed regularly.
6. The oil seals in the slider tend to be vulnerable, particularly on unshrouded forks. Here, there is normally a dust cover to remove – it slips into a groove round the top of the slider – before this large circlip can be winkled out with a screwdriver.
7. Now the oil seal can be prised out – something that should normally only be done when it is faulty, or to give access to a worn bush below it. On reassembly, always fit a new oil seal. Pre-lubricate the seal lips with a smear of grease or damping fluid so that the edges of the stanchion tube pass smoothly through. Assembling the seal dry can allow the tube to cut into the seal, thereby weakening it and producing leakage

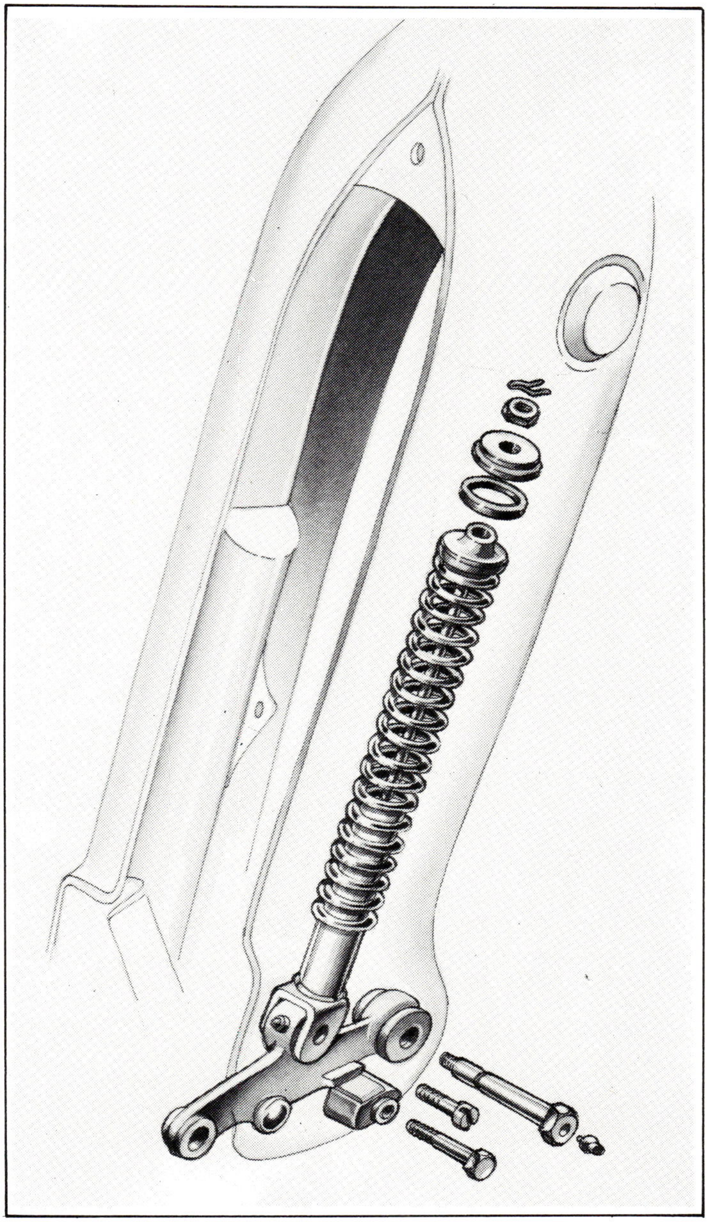

Left: Swinging-link forks are of simple design – each leg is basically a link and a spring/damper unit

Brakes

Increasingly, modern motorcycle practice is to use hydraulically-operated disc brakes for the front wheel, and either a hydraulic disc or mechanically-operated drum brake for the rear wheel. The two systems operate differently.

Mechanical drum brakes

Dealing with the drum brake first, as its name suggests, this consists of a drum formed integrally with the hub, with a shrunk-in ring – usually of cast iron – to form the hard surface on which the brake shoe linings bear.

The shoes themselves, semi-circular in configuration, are of light alloy or steel and carry friction linings on their outer faces. Each shoe is pivoted on a brake plate. In leading-and-trailing shoe designs, both shoes have common pivots. The lower pivot is fixed; the upper pivot is a cam to which is connected the brake operating arm. As the arm is moved the cam turns, and presses the shoes outwards against the resistance of a pair of springs that link the shoe webs. The friction linings of the shoes bear on the inner surface of the drum. When the lever pressure is released, the springs retract and pull the shoes out of contact.

When the brakes are applied, the effect of the revolving drum is to throw the front (leading) shoe into closer engagement, and to throw the rear (trailing) shoe out of engagement. The trailing shoe, therefore, does not contribute fully to the power of the brake. A more powerful brake can be obtained if both shoes are arranged to lead. This is done by placing their pivots diametrically opposite each other, and providing each shoe with its own cam. The result is a 'two-leading-shoe' brake. Here, movement of the drum gives both brake shoes a tendency to wrap around the inner face and so increase the operating pressure – a self-servo action, in which the brakes try to increase their own operating pressure.

They have the disadvantage that they will not work adequately if the direction of rotation is reversed – not usually a serious drawback on a motorcycle – and their self-servo action can lead to unpleasant, and even dangerous, 'grabbing' in humid conditions.

All drum brakes suffer from fade as the surfaces of the drum and the linings heat up. The effect of heat is to make the drum expand away from the shoes, so that the clearance between them constantly increases. In severe cases – heavy use down mountain passes, for example – the condition can become so pronounced that the shoes cannot grip the drum properly. Without adequate friction between the drum and the shoes, the braking effort is drastically reduced. Fading is the visible evidence that this stage has been reached, and the only way to counteract it is to stop and let the brakes cool down.

Hydraulic disc brakes

Disc brakes virtually eliminate fade. Here, the friction linings are pads, that grip the sides of a thin stainless steel or cast-iron disc bolted to the wheel hub. Friction between them again causes heat, and the disc expands. But, this time, the expansion is of no consequence, since the friction surfaces are unaffected by it. The disc can increase its *diameter* as much as it likes, and the pads mounted each side of it will still maintain their original relationship with it. Any slight *lateral* expansion would only increase their grip.

Since the pads are mounted beside the disc, there is a further advantage. Disc rotation has no

This Honda drum brake is of the usual leading-and-trailing shoe design, with twin pull-off springs holding the shoes to a common pivot at one side and to a single cam at the other. The brake lever operates the cam, which in turn presses the shoes outwards against the inner surface of the drum.

Honda's current twin-disc brake arrangement using a sliding caliper assembly and plain stainless-steel discs

The BMW front brake, with its disc drilled to improve rainwater clearance and reduce time-lag in the wet. This is a swinging-caliper brake

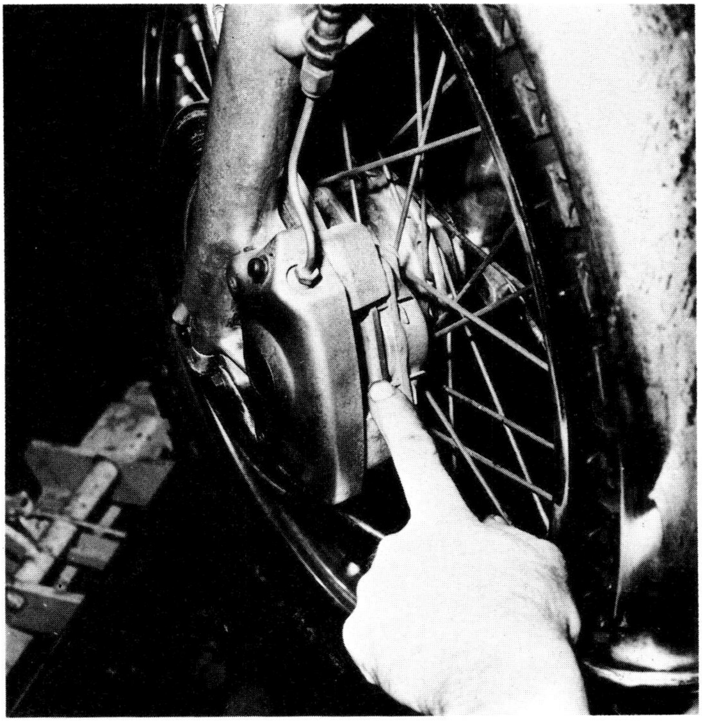

Easy pad inspection of the Lockheed front brake on a Triumph

effect on them, so there is no self-servo effect to cause dangerous 'grabbing'. A disc brake, from the practical riding point of view, responds in exact proportion to the pressure applied through the brake lever.

Most discs are hydraulically operated. The principle here is that fluid is incompressible. Fill a tube with fluid: insert a piston at one end and a piston at the other; and press either piston. The fluid will force the other piston outwards by exactly the amount that you moved the first.

That is precisely how the disc brake is actuated. The master cylinder at the handlebar end is filled with fluid, closed off by a piston operated by the brake lever. The cylinder is linked by a fluid-filled pipe to a chamber in the brake caliper, which again is closed off by a piston. Press the brake lever, and the fluid transmits the force you have applied and presses the caliper piston outwards. On the face of this piston is a pad of friction material, which contacts the disc. Some calipers contain two pistons, with the effort divided between them. It is more usual, however, to use a single piston and to arrange for the reaction of its movement to move the caliper itself so that it brings a second pad into contact with the other side of the disc. The effect, either way, is like pinching a plate between thumb and forefinger.

The piston passes through a rubber seal, which prevents fluid seeping out of the caliper. As the brake is applied, the outward movement of the piston distorts the seal. As soon as the pressure is released, the seal acts like a rubber spring, and pulls the piston back as it reverts to its previous shape, retracting the pads from the disc at the same time.

Hydraulic systems have two

other advantages compared with mechanical operation. The brake is self-adjusting, since the quantity of fluid in the system remains constant by drawing more from its reservoir as the pad wears and the piston moves progressively further out. And, of course, it is self-lubricating.

Some makes of disc brakes have acquired a largely unwarranted bad reputation, based on their undeniable time-lag from application to 'bite' when they are wet. This can be countered by lightly applying the brake every mile, and by making the initial application harder than in the dry. The allowance of three car-lengths extra braking distance should then give an ample safety factor.

Long-term, sintered brake pads developed in Britain should eliminate wet-lag completely.

In practice, it is *drum* brakes that need more care under wet conditions, since they can 'grab' viciously if not properly maintained, and are also prone to locking-up.

Drum brake maintenance

Drum brakes can suffer from three main problems. Squeal and snatch are normally caused by dust, rubbed off the shoes, collecting in the drum. A particularly vicious form of snatch, which is in fact a self-servo action, can sometimes be alleviated by increasing the chamfer on the leading and trailing edges of the shoe. Binding – failure of the brake to release properly – indicates semi-seizure of the operating cam, usually due to neglected lubrication of the spindle.

Remove the wheel, and the brake backplate – complete with shoes and operating mechanism – lifts out. Clean away all dust from the drum – it is best blown out, using a tyre pump – and then wipe

After applying the brakes a few thousand times, brake dust ground off the faces of the linings collects in the brake and can cause noisy and snatchy operation. Always wipe the drum and shoes clean when a brake is dismantled

the drum with methylated spirits.

To remove the shoes, expand them sideways against the pull of their springs, and lift each shoe in turn as it clears the cam or the pivot. Quite a lot of force is needed at times, and while some mechanics believe in applying leverage with a screwdriver, this can be a dangerous proceeding if the tool happens to slip.

Before detaching the shoes, note exactly how the return springs are fitted, since they have to go back the same way round. Then unhook the springs and check the shoes for wear. Renew them as a pair, even though one may be more worn than the other. Modern linings are usually bonded to the shoes, so there is no option to fitting new or exchange shoes. 'Oldies' had linings riveted to the shoes, but ensuring a secure fitting as a DIY job is too tricky to make it a recommendable practice. One mistake could be the last!

Make a point of removing the brake cam so that the spindle can be washed clean in petrol, and then well lubricated with grease before assembly. With age, grease tends to harden and prevent the spindle moving freely, so it pays to be meticulous.

Before offering up the shoes – best done by linking them with the springs and expanding them into position, though it is sometimes easier to leave one spring for later fitting – lubricate the pivot post and the cam with white brake grease. Use this, too, on anti-rattle springs fitted to the shoe webs.

Drum brake adjustment

Adjustment is simple, but often not properly carried out. All drum brake adjustment systems work on the principle of varying the effective length of the operating mechanism. If it is a rod, it is

On older-type drum brakes, shoe lining wear can be judged by the angle of the brake arm. These are at their limit. The arm should angle well back. Later brakes have a wear indicator built on the backplate

To prevent the backplate from revolving when the brake is operated, the torque arm is bolted to the brake backplate at one end, and to the frame at the other. For safety, the securing nut often has a spring circlip. This must always be securely replaced

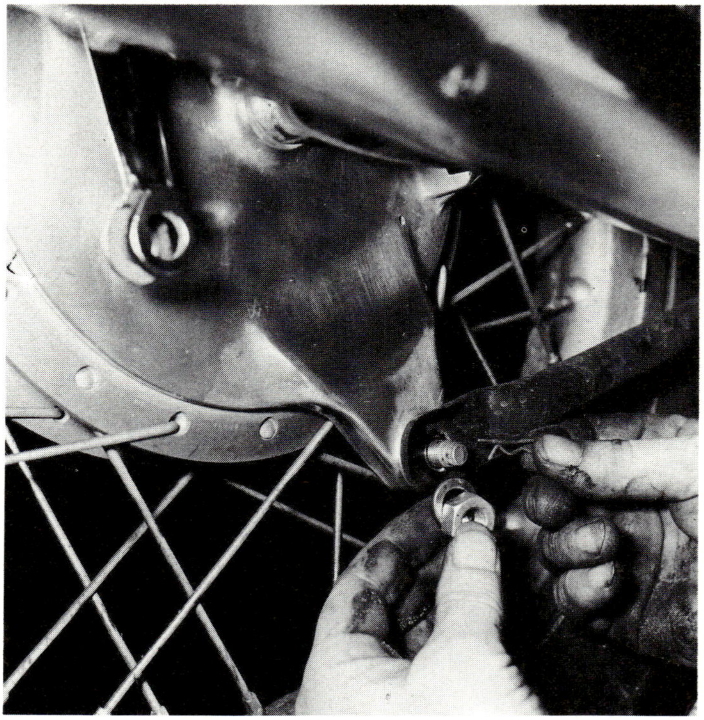

threaded, and its thrust is transmitted to the brake arm through a shaped nut bearing on a clevis pin, through which the rod passes. With cables, the adjustment is the familiar cable-adjuster system, sometimes duplicated at the handlebar end to permit the front brake setting to be varied on the move.

It is best, however, always to adjust a brake with the weight off the wheel, so that it can be spun. Take up the adjustment until you can hear the brake shoes starting to rub on the drum. Then ease off until they are just out of contact again. Check that this setting gives the requisite free play at the pedal or the lever recommended by the manufacturer. Usually, this is between three-quarters of an inch and an inch of movement at the brake pedal pad or the end of the handlebar lever. Reset the adjustment accordingly.

Sometimes overlooked is the provision of an adjustment for brake pedal position. This usually takes the form of a screwed stop with a locknut, bearing on the upper side of the brake pedal. Free off the brake adjustment, and release the locknut. Screw the stop up or down until the pedal pad rests neatly under your foot (remember that if you ride in boots the adjustment must be made with the thickness of the boot sole in mind) and then tighten the locknut. Reset the brake adjustment, and also check that the new setting has not interfered with the 'timing' of the brake light. The switch for this has an adjuster built in, too. Raising the switch body brings the light on sooner; lowering it delays its operation. Just loosen the appropriate nut, and take up or release the other until the timing of the lamp is right. Then lock up again.

Some twin leading-shoe brakes – the Jawa pattern, for instance –

A typical rear brake rod arrangement. The rod is spring-loaded, so that as the adjuster nut is tightened it is firmly held on the trunnion. The nut has its face radiused to mate with the trunnion, so that it can only be set in half-turns. For rear wheel removal, the nut has to be removed, and the brake must then be readjusted on assembly

require the shoes to be independently adjusted. The sequence with these is to slacken off the linking rod. Free play at the handlebars is then set by use of the normal cable adjuster, and then the linking rod is set by tightening its adjuster nut until the shoes begin to bind on the drum. At that point, the nut is backed off by one to one and a half turns to restore free rotation, and the new setting is held by tightening the locknut on the rod.

Care of cables

The brake mechanism includes the cables and levers used to control it. Cables require periodic lubrication, and this is best done by running in a 'thick' petrol/oil mixture. Free off the cable adjustment, so that the upper end of the outer casing can be eased from its abutment on the lever. Turn the nipple in its housing till the cable aligns with its cutaway, and pull it out of engagement.

Now make up a small 'funnel' by moulding Plasticine round the mouth of the outer casing. Make up a small quantity of petroil – say about 8 parts of petrol to one of oil – and tie the cable to the bars so the funnel is uppermost. Run the petroil into the funnel. It will penetrate through the length of the cable casing, and as the petrol evaporates you will be left with a film of oil all down the cable. Note, however, that this method should *not* be used on cables that already have an anti-friction lining to their outers.

The exposed sections of cable and the nipples and lever pivots should all be lightly lubricated with grease, and a constant check should be kept on the action at the lever ends. The nipples must rotate freely in their housings as the brake is operated, so giving a straight pull on the cable. If the

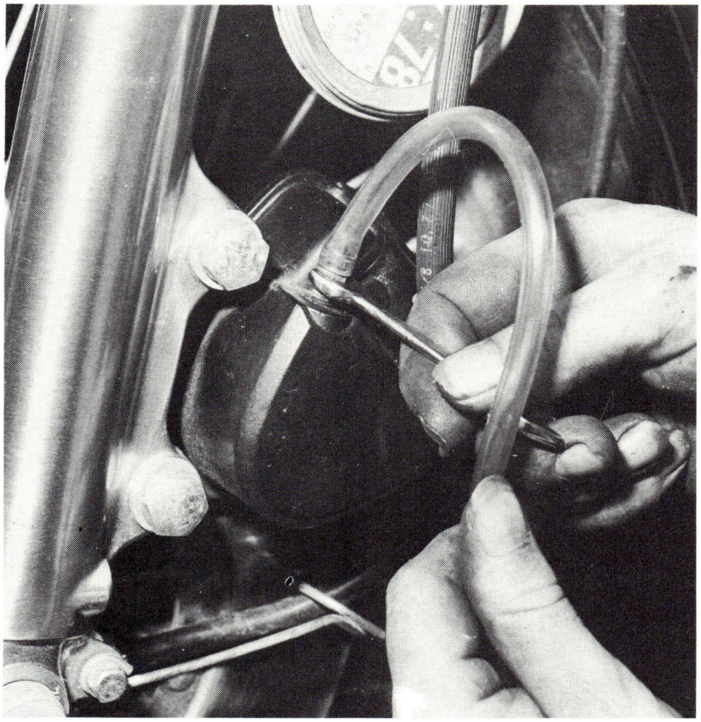

Disc brakes need to be bled of air if any has entered the hydraulic system and is causing spongy operation. Brake bleeding is an easy job as explained in the text

nipple binds, the cable will be bent from side to side each time it operates, and like any other piece of metal that is subjected to such treatment it soon suffers from metal fatigue and snaps.

Care of hydraulic systems

With hydraulic operation used on the majority of disc brakes, adjustment is automatic. Even brake bleeding – expelling air from the system – only needs to be done if by some chance air has entered. This can only happen if there is leakage, if the fluid level in the reservoir has been allowed to fall, or if a connection has been loosened.

The first step in caring for the system, therefore, is to keep a regular check on the security of all connections and on the level in the reservoir. The hoses, too, must be carefully looked at each week for signs of cuts or abrasions – even though they are of armoured construction.

If air enters the system, the control soon begins to feel soggy. Pumping it usually restores its normal operation for a while, but it will not cure the trouble.

To bleed the air, you need a length of transparent plastic hose that will fit tightly over the bleed screw and reach down to ground level. You also need a jar, and a tin of brake fluid.

Put the bike on its stand so the reservoir is upright. Take off the cap, remove the diaphragm that is usually fitted inside, and top up the reservoir to the Maximum mark. Then refit the cap.

Remove the cover from the bleed screw, and press the hose over the orifice. Pour about an inch of fluid into the jar, and immerse the end of the hose in it. That prevents air being drawn up into the system when the bleed screw is opened.

Though you can do this job single-handed, it helps to have an assistant at this point. The brake lever has to be operated hard and then, with the pressure still held on, the bleed screw must be opened by half a turn. As the lever moves to its stop, a jet of fluid will be expelled into the hose, and the bleed screw must be closed just as the lever completes its travel. When the screw is home again, release the lever. Now repeat the sequence – apply pressure; open the bleed screw; let the lever move to the end of its travel; close the bleed screw; release the lever. This will have to be done four or five times before you again remove the reservoir cap and top up the fluid.

Keep repeating the sequence until the fluid issuing from the system is free of air bubbles. Then lock down the bleed screw and remove the hose. Refit the bleed screw cap; top up the reservoir again and refit the diaphragm and cap.

Never use the fluid from the jar – it will be contaminated. Fill only with fresh fluid from your tin, and keep the tin sealed between times.

Some manufacturers – they include Suzuki – recommend changing the brake fluid every year. Brake fluid is hygroscopic – it attracts water, which can actually permeate through the flexible brake hoses to contaminate the fluid. Water in the system heats up under braking, and can form vapour locks which destroy the efficiency of the brakes. A complete fluid change guards against this, and it is easy to carry out.

Proceed in just the same way as for bleeding, except that you simply open the bleed screw and operate the brake lever to pump the existing fluid out of the system. Obviously, a small amount will still be trapped, but not sufficient to make any difference.

Top up the reservoir with fresh fluid, and pump until this new fluid appears at the bleed screw. Then lock the screw down, top up again, and bleed the system in the normal way.

Pad changing

Apart from brake bleeding, pad changing is the only recommended DIY job that should be carried out on hydraulic disc braking systems. The reason for this reservation is that hydraulics are extremely sensitive to dirt, that the working surfaces of the cylinders are machined to very fine tolerances and standards of finish, and that only a professional workshop has the tools and expertise to ensure that any internal work on the system is carried out to the requisite safety standards.

Changing pads is a reasonably straightforward job that varies mainly in the requirements inherent in the different caliper designs. One point in common with all of them, though, is that to do the job the operating pistons have to be pressed back into their housings, and this may cause the reservoir to overflow, with disastrous results on paintwork. Watch the level, therefore, and if necessary siphon off the excess fluid as the work proceeds. Then discard it. It is never to be re-used.

Swinging calipers

Honda are the largest users of swinging calipers, which also feature on BMWs. With this type of brake, the caliper unit is pivoted about a pin, and there is only one hydraulic piston. As this is operated, reaction causes the caliper to swing, bringing a static shoe into contact with the opposite side of the disc.

To change pads on Honda swinging-caliper brakes the front

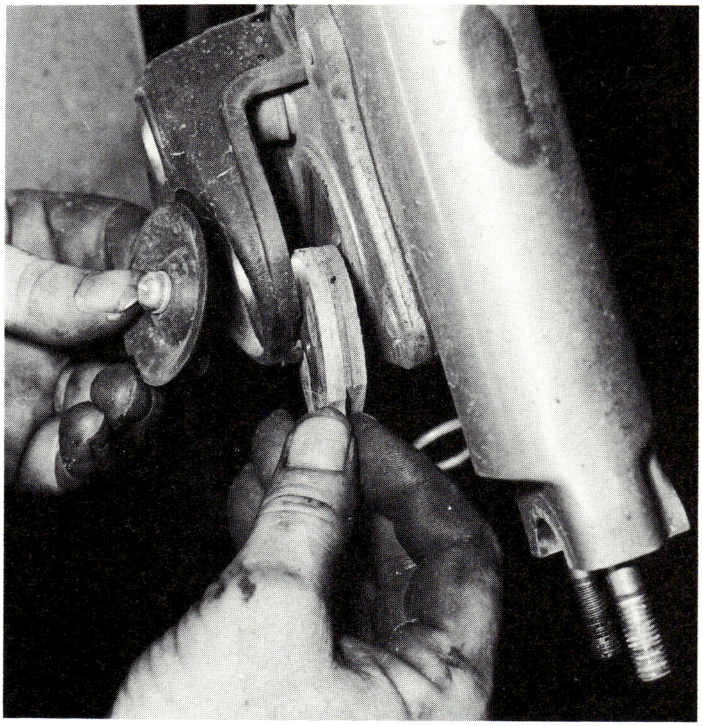

Pad Removal on the Suzuki GS400
(1) The fixed pad is held in the housing by this plate and screw. It is removed first

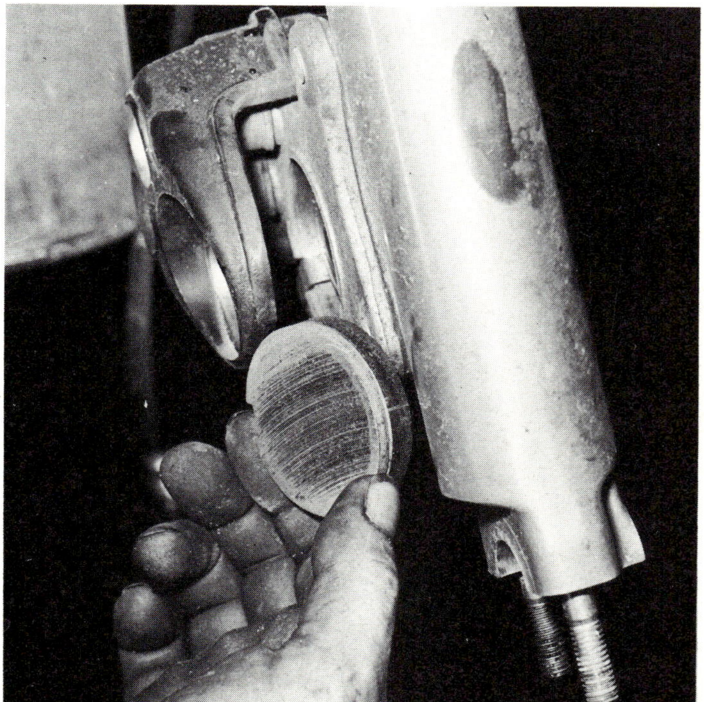

Pad Removal on the Suzuki GS400
(2) Then the pad that is moved by the hydraulic piston is slipped out of its housing

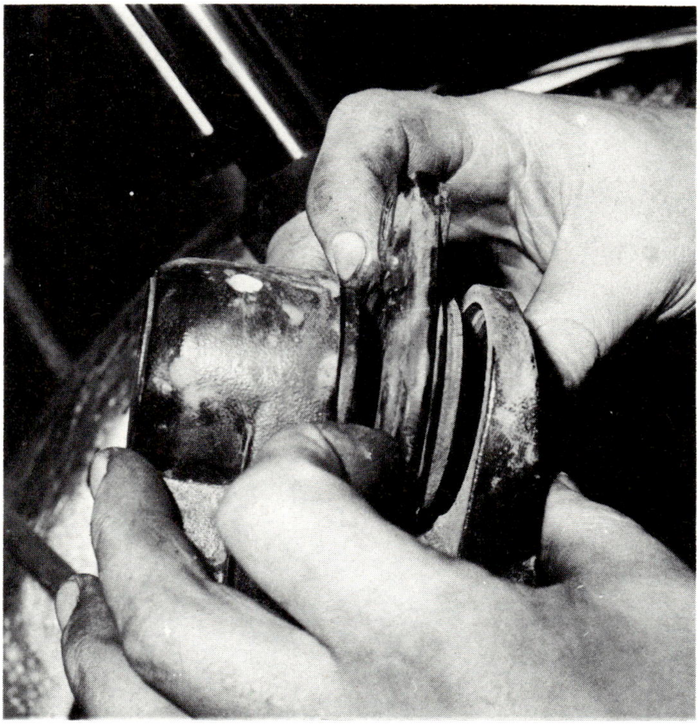

On the Suzuki 1000, the caliper is freed from the fork first. The fixed pad is removed as before: the moving pad is wiggled out through the hole in the caliper mounting

Rear disc brakes often have these square-type pads. The shims on the back must not be omitted when fitting new pads

The earlier-type Honda disc brake is easy to dismantle. The fixed pad is held to this bolted-on carrier. . .

. . .by a single split pin, which simply prevents it from tilting towards the disc

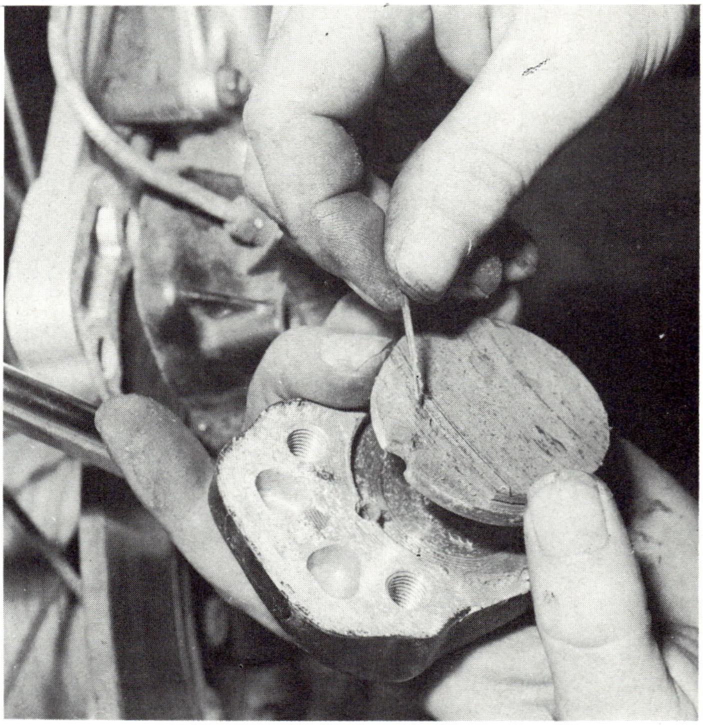

wheel is first removed by releasing the spindle clamps. Once the wheel is out, the brake lever must *not* be operated, or the piston will be displaced from the caliper.

Two through-bolts hold the caliper halves together. Free them, and detach the inner (static) pad, which is held in place by a split-pin. The outer pad, on which the piston bears, just lifts out.

The projecting section of the steel piston must now be cleaned – a job best done with rag and methylated spirits. Get rid of all road dirt, and then press the piston firmly back into its housing.

Now apply a sparing coat of silicon-based grease to the back of the steel pad backing plates, and very carefully wipe a film of grease over the edges too. Do not let any of it get on to the friction material itself. Slip the moving pad into place on the piston, and fit the static pad to the retainer, using a new split-pin.

It is usually possible to ease the disc into place between the new pads, so refit the static pad retainer and then offer up the wheel. If the disc tends to displace the pads, however, the retainer can be left loose until the wheel is in position, and then tightened up.

Now, the clearance between the inner pad and the disc has to be accurately measured. It must be precisely 0·15 mm (0·0059 in) and it is adjusted by resetting the spring-loaded horizontal adjuster bolt on the caliper arm. Some troubles with Honda front brakes are attributable to this adjustment having been overlooked, and another potential fault is semi-seizure of the caliper on its pivot pin. This should be periodically removed, cleaned, and greased.

On the BMW swinging caliper, the static pad is held in place by a spring clip engaged with a pair of lugs. After detaching the wheel, removal of the clip frees the static pad, while the moving pad engages in a spigot in the piston and can be pulled out of place.

Again, the piston must have its projecting area cleaned before it is pressed back into the housing.

BMW pads are tapered, and in each case the leading edge is straight while the trailing edge is curved. The pads cannot be confused, and there is nothing unusual about refitting them except the need to lubricate the 'O' ring on the piston pad with a little Molykote BR-2.

The setting-up, however, is unusual. The disc has to be wire brushed to remove any dirt or corrosion around its edges, and after the wheel has been refitted there is an alignment sequence that must be carried out.

At the base of the caliper pivot pin is a screwed cap. Detach this, and take out the spring inside the pivot. Now use a felt-tipped pen to draw radial lines across the inner face of the disc. Spin the wheel, and while it is rotating grasp the caliper body and pull it outwards so that the inner pad rubs on the disc. Examine the ink marks: they should be rubbed evenly away. Adjustment is made by inserting a screwdriver from below, and turning the pivot pin, which is eccentrically mounted. Re-check the adjustment in the same way, and when the necessary even contact has been achieved refit the spring and cap.

The brake lever can then be operated to press the pads up against the disc face. Afterwards remove the fuel tank and use the specially-supplied feeler gauge in the BMW tool kit to check that the setting of the control cable between the master cylinder and the lever is correct. The only adjustment possible here is the familiar screw-action alteration of the effective length of the cable.

A variation on the reaction-caliper system is the sliding unit used by Kawasaki and Suzuki.

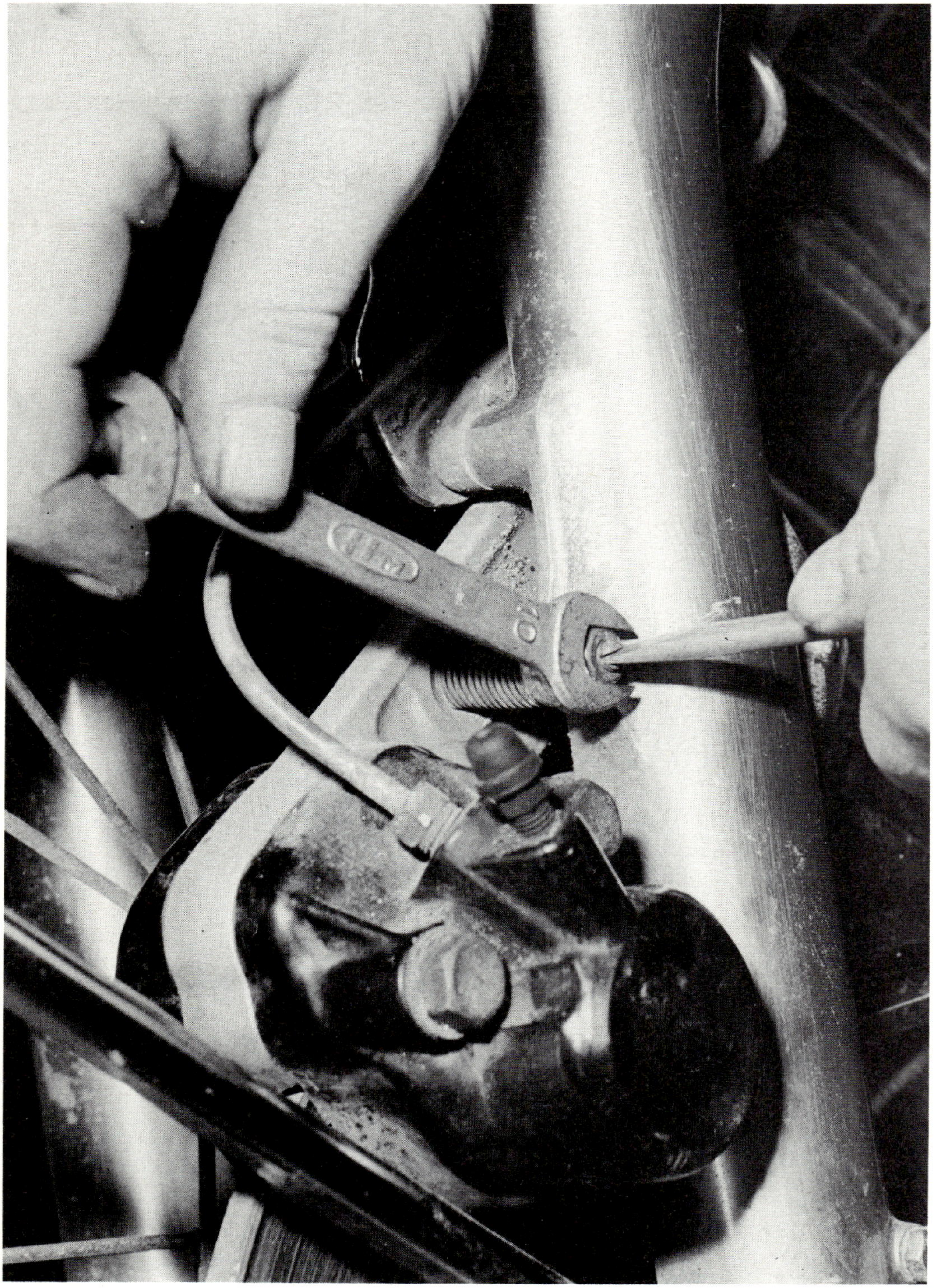

Again, pad changing starts by removing the front wheel after detaching the spindle clamps, and the inner pad is then freed by removing a single cross-headed screw on the housing's inner face. Where Suzuki differ is in using the pressure in the hydraulic system to eject the other pad. The brake lever must be squeezed – very gently indeed – until the pad has been pressed through the access hole in the pad mounting plate. It can then be lifted from the caliper.

If this technique were to be used on any of the models with twin disc brakes, there would be a considerable danger of one piston also being ejected from the second brake. Therefore, a spacer of the same width as the disc has to be inserted into one caliper and this remains there while all the work is carried out on the other. When it is complete, the spacer is transferred to the first caliper, and the operations are repeated.

With the Suzuki twin-disc arrangement, one caliper must be detached before the wheel can be removed. The pipework is not touched, other than to free the hose guide on that side. The caliper is simply lifted, and tied to the fork temporarily. When the wheel is off, the caliper is refitted.

British practice is exemplified by the double-piston caliper used on the Norton Commando. Here, the caliper is solidly mounted and each pad is operated independently by its own piston. This, of course, complicates matters slightly, since access space is limited. Once the wheel has been removed, dislodge the pads and then use a small soft brush to clean the pistons from below. That done, clean up the old pads, temporarily refit them, and insert a large screwdriver between them. Work this from side to side to press the pistons back into the caliper, keeping a careful eye on the fluid level in the reservoir as you do so – as previously mentioned, brake fluid damages paintwork.

With the pistons home, dislodge the old pads again and offer up the new ones, having first smeared the back of each with Lockheed disc brake lubricant.

The earliest disc brakes – the first on a motorcycle were introduced by Maserati in 1956 – were cable operated, and a few non-hydraulic units are still used, notably on some of the Honda lightweights. Pad changing on these is a rather different operation, since there is a self-adjustment mechanism to reset.

When the wheel has been detached, the caliper cover is removed by detaching three bolts. Beneath it is a thrust assembly, which is swung to one side. The outer pad is then removed by screwing into it one of the cover-mounting bolts, gripping it, and pulling. The other pad is located by a pin. Just push it in, and the pad will come away quite easily.

Before the new pads can be fitted, the self-adjusting mechanism must be set. One end of the mechanism terminates in a thrust button which bears on the outer pad; the other has a plastic ratchet wheel. Lift this wheel out and insert a screwdriver into the self-adjuster. Wind the adjustment back and refit the wheel.

Grease the backs of the new pads, and the sides of the outer pad 'piston', using silicon-based grease. Take care not to get any grease on the pad lining. Refit the two pads – they are so dissimilar that it is impossible to mix them up – and set up the outer pad so that the pin on the thrust mechanism fits in such a way that the thrust ring is aligned with its slots. Refit the cover, replace the wheel, and adjust the brake by operating the brake lever until all play is taken up.

Opposite: The swinging arm on this Honda brake is equipped with a spring-loaded adjuster. This is set to give a clearance of 0·15 mm between the inner caliper pad and the disc

Routine maintenance

The guide to be followed for the jobs required on your particular bike is the Owner's Handbook supplied with the machine. This sets out the checks and operations that need to be carried out, and gives the elapsed mileage basis on which to work. Replacement books can usually be ordered through a dealer when the original has gone astray.

Although the elapsed-mileage system is a sound one, it does mean keeping an accurate log of the mileometer readings at which any jobs were actually done. It is not safe to rely on memory. Was the oil last changed at 15,600 miles or 16,500 miles for instance, you may wonder, and with some engines oil-change periods exceeding the maker's intervals by no more than 1,500 miles can mean a prematurely worn motor rather than a long-lived one.

Take a typical routine-maintenance sequence for one of the current 'fours' as an example:

Every 300 miles: Lubricate the final drive chain.

Every 500 miles: Adjust the final drive chain.

Every 2,000 miles: Drain the sump and refill with fresh oil.

Every 3,000 miles: Change the oil filter element. Clean the air filter element. Clean the sparking plugs. Adjust the cam chain. Adjust the rear brake. Grease the swinging-arm pivot bushes.

Check all the following points. – Contact-breaker gaps; ignition timing; tappet clearances; carburettor adjustment; throttle operation; fuel tank tap and pipes; clutch adjustment; fluid level in front brake hydraulic reservoir; front disc brake pads; front brake hoses and pipes; rear brake rod linkages; wheel rims; wheel spokes; tyres; stand springs; lights, horn, instruments; battery electrolyte.

Every 6,000 miles: Change the air filter element. Drain the oil from the front forks and refill with fresh lubricant.

Check the following points. – Engine oil pressure; adjustment of steering head bearings; operation of the steering lock; rear brake shoes.

Every 12,000 miles: Remove the sump pan and clean the mesh strainer on the oil pump.

A formidable list even at first glance, and daunting when the sheer weight of book-keeping needed to carry it out is considered. However, allowing that an average annual mileage is something like 6,000 miles, the complete sequence will take two years to complete. In 24 months, the 300-mile job will need to be carried out 40 times; the 500-mile job 24 times; the 2,000-mile work six times; the 3,000-mile tasks four times; the 6,000-mile list, twice; and the 12,000-mile one, once. That makes 77 operations to be logged if the schedule is to be kept, which many riders will be unable to do.

Not all machines are as complicated as an ohc 'four', of course; but the routine jobs even on a simple two-stroke can add up to quite a list:

Every 2,000 miles: Clean and gap the sparking plug. Clean the air filter. Adjust the throttle cable. Adjust the idling speed. Drain the transmission, and refill with fresh oil. Adjust the clutch cable. Lubricate the final drive chain. Adjust the final drive chain. Adjust the front brake. Adjust the rear brake. Tighten the cylinder head nuts. Grease all nipples. Oil all cables.

Check the following points. – Contact-breaker gap; ignition timing; battery electrolyte level; battery specific gravity; petrol filter; spokes; all nuts and bolts.

Every 4,000 miles: Decarbonise the cylinder head and piston crown. Decarbonise the exhaust port, exhaust pipe, and tail pipe. Wash and lubricate the final drive chain. Grease the brake operating cams. Remove the float chamber for cleaning.

Given an annual mileage of 4,000 miles, the 2,000-mile jobs would be repeated twice and the 4,000-mile jobs would need to be done once, making nearly 50 operations to be logged.

Though you may start out with the best of intentions, almost certainly something will be overlooked – perhaps a complete maintenance sequence – and the bike suffers. That is why it is better to use a system of running maintenance, such as that employed by many police forces to keep their machines in first-class order.

The police method is based on constant checks. First, there is the

A routine job on many modern two-strokes – checking the setting of the throttle-controlled oil pump. On the Jawa it is mounted beneath a cover plate and the setting is checked by ensuring that the notch on the cable drum is no more than 1·5 mm below the line cast on the pump body. It is adjusted by slackening the cable completely, and then tightening until the marks line up

simple one that every police patrolman carries out before he takes his bike out on to the road at the start of his shift. A typical preriding check is:

Verify fuel and oil levels. Visually check the tyre treads. Check the tyre sidewalls for damage. Check the tyre pressures. Test the final drive chain tension. Check the setting and operation of the rear suspension. Check the steering head for play. Test the lights, flashers, and horn. Check the 'feel' of the controls. On moving off, test both brakes.

This five-minute check-up virtually ensures that the bike cannot go on to the road in a faulty state, but it is reinforced by a further routine by which police riders set great store. Each bike is cleaned thoroughly, every week.

Dirt can hide faults, and to get rid of dirt a rider has to touch and inspect the whole exterior of the bike. Thus this cleaning session has a double purpose: to keep the bike looking smart, and to keep it safe and efficient. During the cleaning, every nut and bolt is checked for security, and every spoke for tension. The frame is checked for cracks; the forks and rear spring units for tell-tale signs of oil that give warning of an internal seal failure.

Lastly, police bikes go into the workshop for a complete check at 2,000-mile intervals. This is often on a stem-to-stern basis, the inspection and servicing starting at the front wheel and ending at the rear light. A typical workshop routine would be:

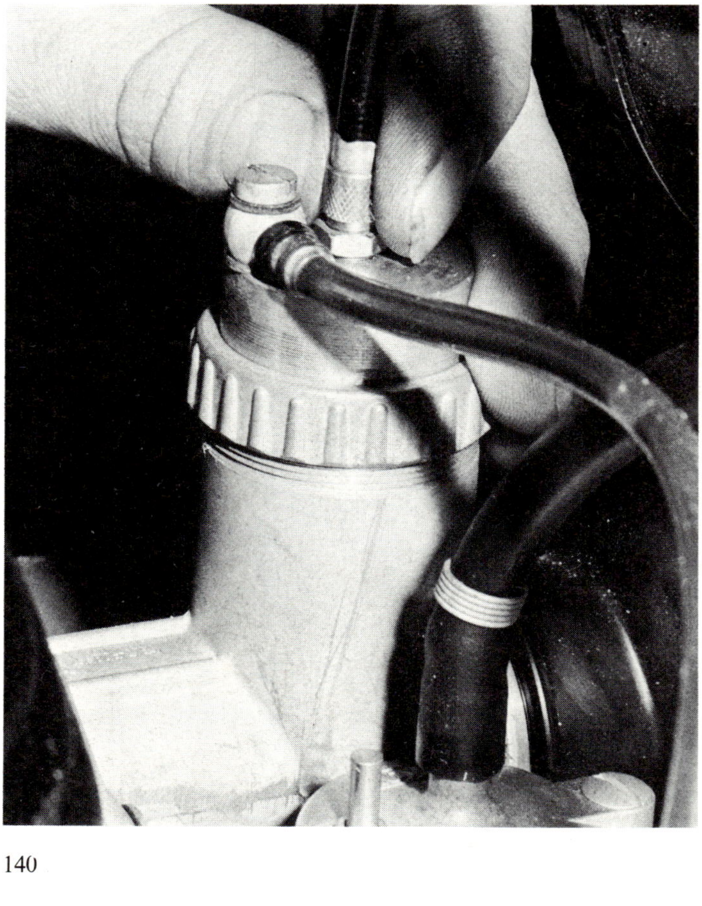

With the Jawa's oiling system, a second cable from the oil pump drum runs to the throttle slide. This is adjusted by screwing it out a few turns, then screwing it back again until the slide can be heard to hit the carburettor body when the throttle control is opened and released

Front wheel. – Examine the tyre sidewall for cuts, cracks, or other damage. Check the tread depths. Remove trapped stones. Check the tread area for cuts or damage. Check the tyre valve for air leakage. Check the valve securing nut. Check the valve cap. Examine the rims for damage or distortion. Check all spokes for security (maximum adjustment possible on nipple without removing tyre to grind down spoke protrusion, half a turn). Lift or remove wheel to check bearings. Test the bearings for side play. Check the condition of the spindle. Check the spindle clamps and bolts for security. Check the speedometer drive gearbox and cable. Check the front brake disc and securing bolts.

Front forks. – Rock forks to check for play in the sliders and the steering head. Block the front wheel clear of the ground and check the forks for free movement on to each lock. Change the fork oil if due (maximum elapsed mileage, 10,000 miles). Check all mudguard fastenings for security.

Front brake. – Check pad wear on discs, or adjustment on drum-brake systems. Check all hydraulic lines, or brake cables, for deterioration. Verify hydraulic fluid level. At 15,000 miles maximum, pump out all old fluid; flush system; refill, and bleed.

Headlamp group. – Test for setting. Inspect reflector and renew if dulled. Check headlamp and flasher bulbs, and renew any on which glass envelope is discoloured. Check wiring for loose connections. Also check wiring

Japanese machines usually have dipsticks: the Jawa has a level plug for the gearbox oil. Level plugs are used by placing the bike on the stand, and then tilting it slightly towards you. Oil should flow out, showing that internally it is just up to the level of the hole

leads for damaged insulation.

Handlebars. – Check bar clamps for security. Test all controls.

Engine. – Carry out full service – tappets, plugs, contact-breaker points, carburettor adjustment, oil and filter changes as required. Examine all joints for leakage. Check all nuts and bolts.

Tank. – Check taps, filters, fuel leads. Check filler cap. Check tank fastenings.

Suspension. – Examine pivot bearing. Lubricate bearing and check pivot for security. Check spring units for leakage. Check upper and lower spring unit fastenings.

Seat. – Check securing bolts and hinges. Check and lubricate seat lock.

Transmission. – Remove, wash, and lubricate final drive chain. Check sprockets. Refit and tension chain. Before refitting, verify security of spring-link roller pins.

Battery. – Remove battery and wash casing. Clean battery terminals. Check specific gravity of cells. Top up with distilled water. Clean contact surfaces of battery leads. Refit battery, coating terminals and leads with Vaseline before remaking connections. Check the fuses and fuse holders. Make sure the battery vent pipe is unblocked and has a clear run.

Stands. – Check stand pivot bolts. Examine stand legs for cracks. Unhook and check stand springs.

Footrests. – Examine for cracks. Check securing bolts. Renew damaged rubbers.

Rear brake. – With discs, check and service as front brake. With drums, check adjustment. Examine brake rod or cable, and lubricate. Check security of brake pedal. Check operation of stop-lamp and adjust switch as necessary.

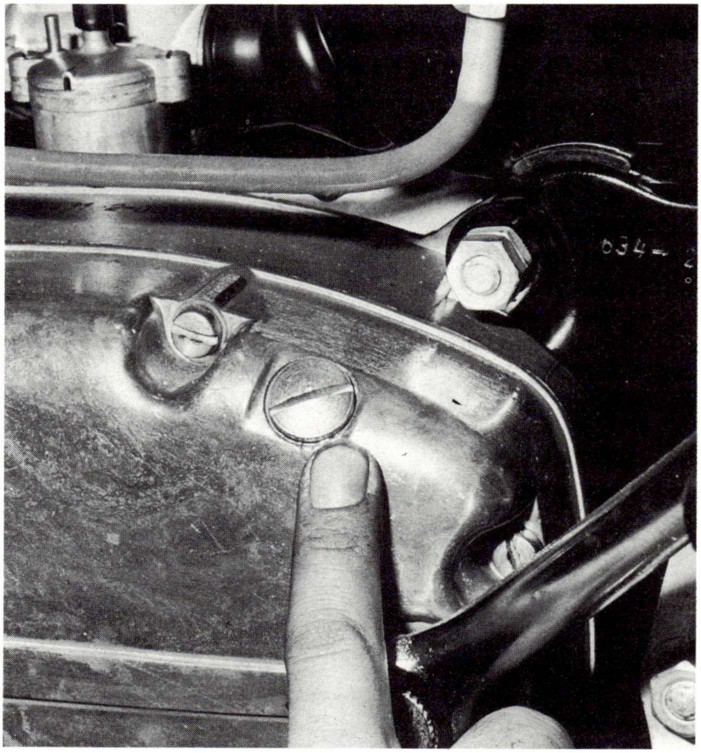

Topping-up is done after removing the combined filler and level plug. Give the oil level a few seconds to rise each time you pour in the oil. When the level is correct, refit the plugs.

On bikes with dipsticks, check the handbook to ascertain if the level should be checked with the plug screwed fully home, or just resting on the rim

Rear wheel. – Check as for front wheel, plus verification of condition of cush-drive hub if fitted.

Rear tyre. – Check as for front tyre.

Rear mudguard. – Check all fastenings. Check rear number plate for security and legibility. Check rear lamp bulb and lens. Check rear flashers, lenses and bulbs. Check all electrical connections.

Ancillary equipment. – Examine for cracks or loose fittings.

Exhaust system. – Check attachment at cylinder head. Examine all pipe and silencer brackets. Check all nuts and bolts for security. Examine silencers for damage to baffles or holes in the silencer walls.

Depending on the system of the garage concerned, a service such as this carried out with the aid of a check-sheet devised for whatever model is being worked on, and each item is ticked off as the individual checks and adjustments are made. Oil and filter changes are noted, with the recorded mileage, so that there is a complete record of the bike's mechanical history. Easy to carry out, and undeniably thorough, it is an ideal system for a dedicated biker who wants to keep his machine in first-class running order all the year round.

Routine maintenance on a twin two-stroke

Servicing procedures vary from bike to bike, but the accompanying photographic sequence of maintenance operations on the Jawa 350 cc two-stroke motor are generally applicable to other two-stroke engines. Some of the rolling chassis operations also apply to other European machines, but not to Japanese models.

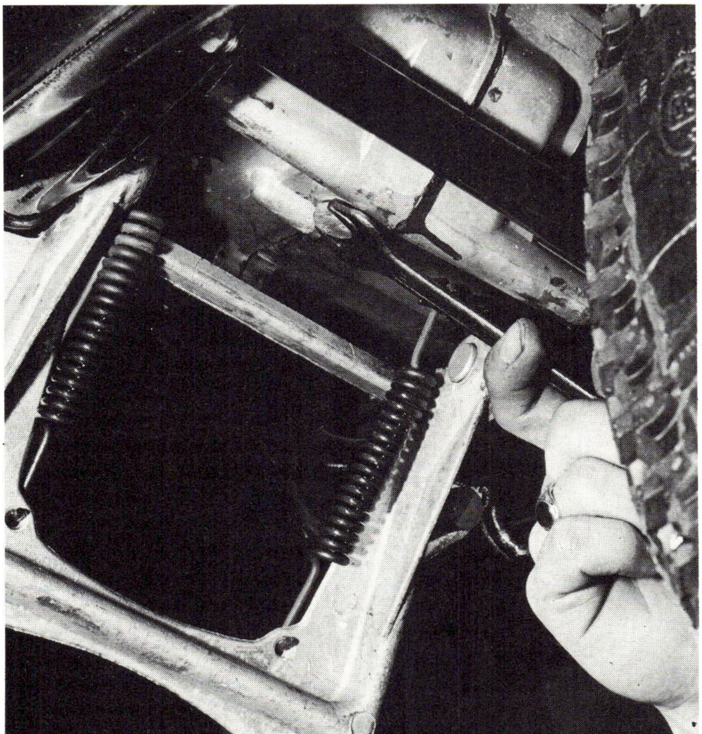

Drain the gearbox oil, after warming up the unit, by removing both this drain plug and the filler plug. Jawa recommend the use of flushing oil to get rid of all deposits – not usually necessary on Japanese bikes. To flush a gearbox, refit the drain plug and fill to the normal level with flushing oil. Run the motor for 10 minutes, changing gear frequently. Then drain thoroughly, and refill with the normal gearbox lubricant – in this case, hypoid 90 oil

Changing the fork oil is necessary on all machines. Some have external fork drain plugs: the Jawa's are concealed by the front wheel spindle, which means the wheel must come out. First, undo the clamp bolt; disconnect the brake cable; and remove the wheel spindle nut. Tap out the spindle

Here is a front fork 10 mm hexagon drain plug. Variations on other models include socket screws; cross-headed screws; or slotted screws. Remove, and allow the oil to drain

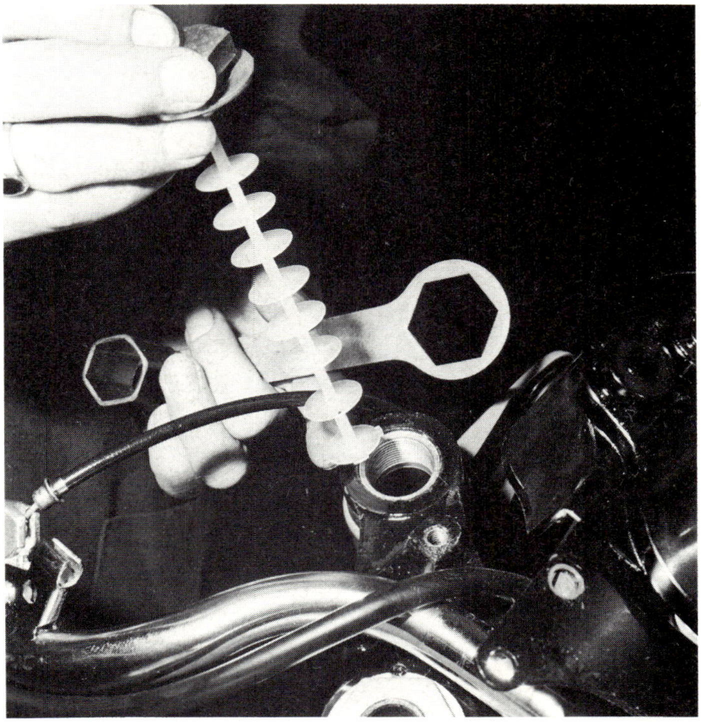

Detach the fork leg plugs. The Jawa is unusual in having baffles. On bikes with Ceriani-type forks, the plugs also act as spring abutments, and the spring will pop up through the aperture. With these, it is better to work on one fork leg at a time

The Jawa's two-leading-shoe front brake assembly, showing the twin operating cams and the two opposed pivots. To remove the shoes, spring them off as shown here. To grease the spindles, remove the spindle nuts and take out one cam at a time. Expand the shoes when refitting them to the backplate

Special to East European bikes is the need to periodically change the rear damper oil. West European and Japanese dampers are sealed units, and cannot be serviced in this way. Damper removal is also different. Japanese bikes have welded-in upper spring anchorages; the Jawa uses a 19 mm bolt

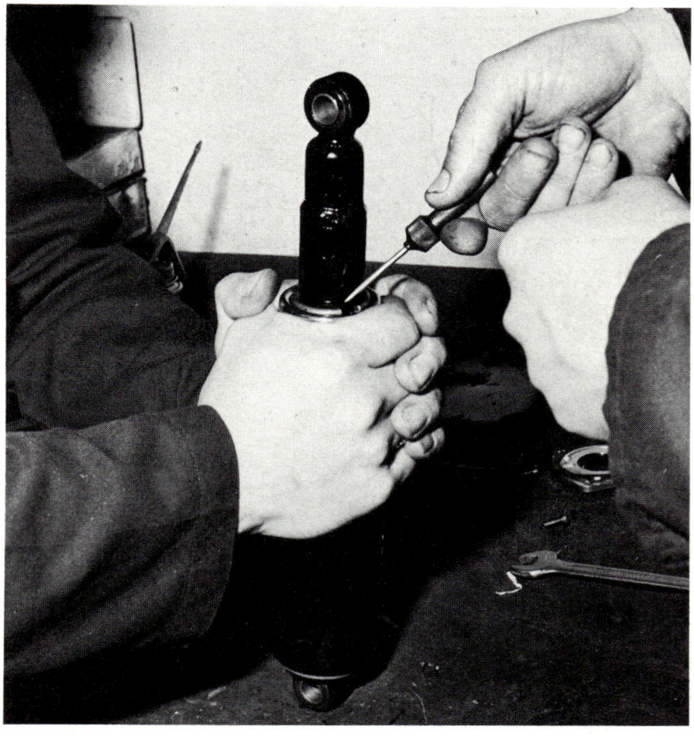

Dismantling the Jawa damper calls for two pairs of hands. One holds the damper compressed, upside down, while the other flicks out the collets

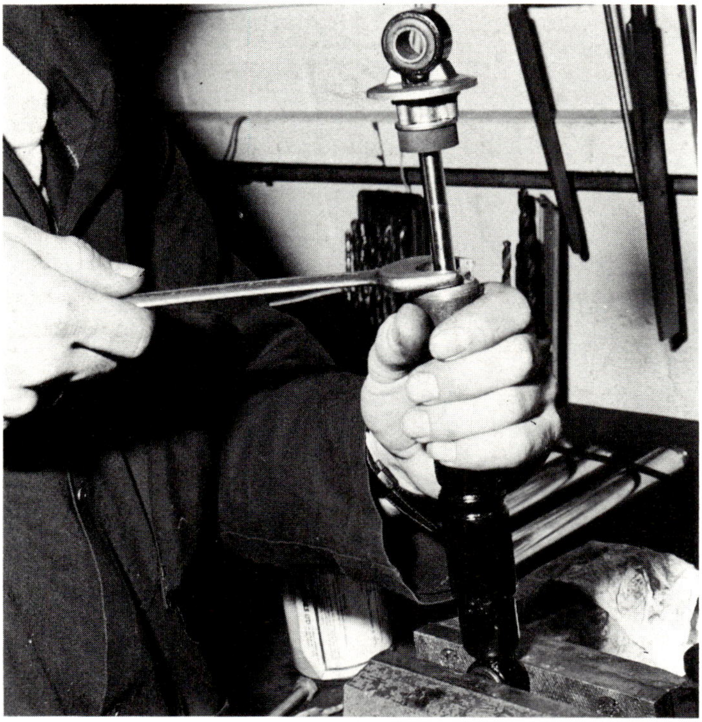

The damper is now withdrawn from the road spring, clamped in a vice, and the damper nut undone to allow the piston to pull out. The oil can then be drained, and the damper topped up with 47 ml of fresh fluid

To reach this casing screw on the Jawa, the rear brake pedal has to have its adjustment slackened off to enable it to clear the screwdriver. Always look for hidden snags such as this when servicing a bike – knowing them can save time, and perhaps prevent damage to components

Not many generators nowadays have carbon brushes, although BMW are one of the more notable exceptions. Spring clips hold the brushes, which should be withdrawn from their holders and checked for condition and wear. They must be at least 6 mm long

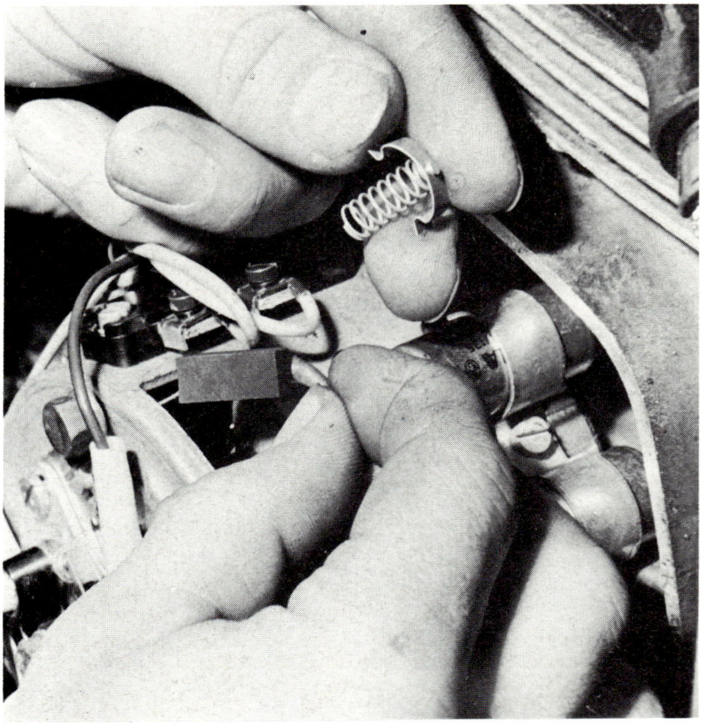

The brushes slide back into their holders quite easily. Jawa brushes have a chamfer on the upper edge, which must face inwards towards the engine

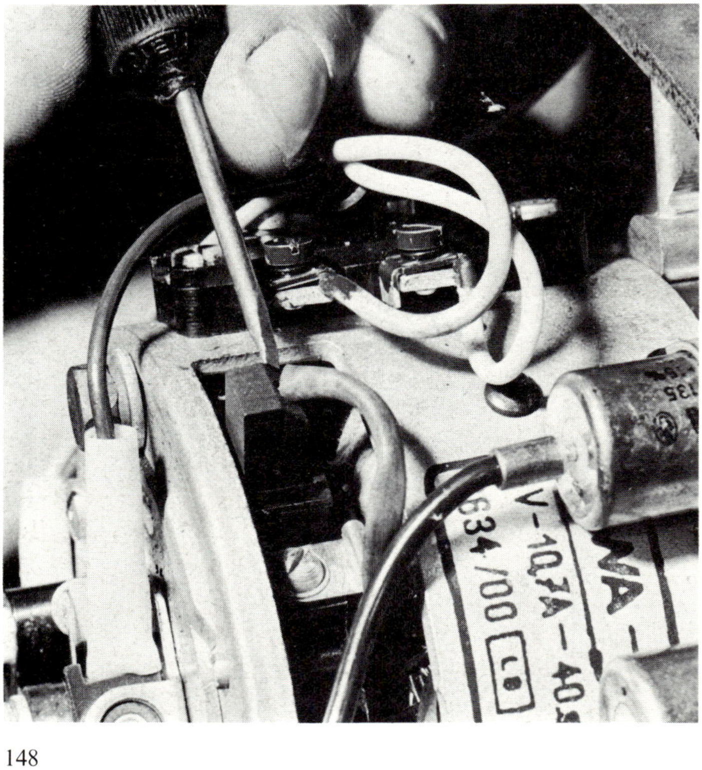

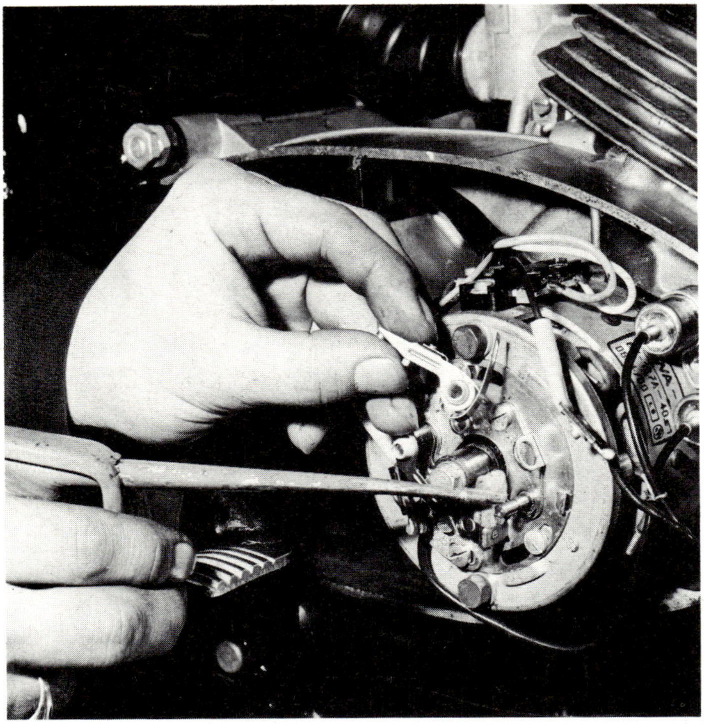

Top Left: Contact-breaker points should be checked, and any piling filed flat. It is better to remove the points arm to do this. At the same time, oil the cam felt

Above: For setting the timing, Jawa recommend use of this gauge, which screws into the plug hole. A similar system, using a dial gauge, is employed on Japanese two-strokes. Two-stroke ignition timing is critical for maximum performance

Left: The gauge is screwed into the plug hole, and the engine is turned over by using a spanner on the dynamo rotor nut. Feeling the plunger of the gauge as the motor is turned, you can establish TDC with accuracy

Checking and resetting the points gap with a feeler gauge follows conventional practice. Loosen the fixed point clamping screw just enough to allow the plate to move under pressure when a screwdriver is used as a lever in the slot. Retighten the clamp, and then check the gap again. On the Jawa, it must be between 0·3 and 0·4 mm. Then repeat the setting procedure on the other set of points

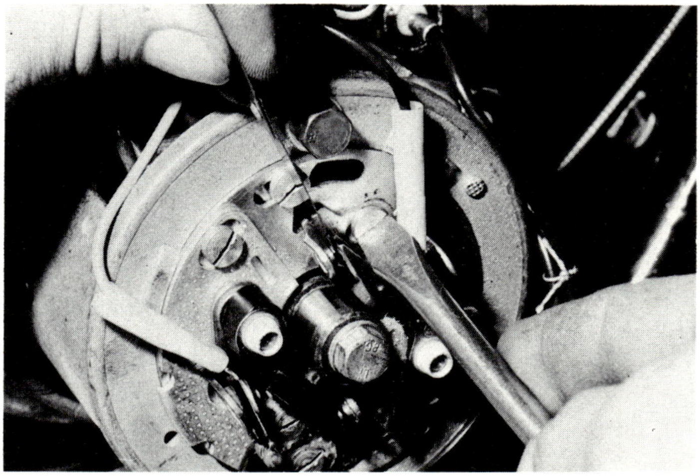

The timing gauge and a piece of cigarette paper will provide a good check on the timing. Set the piston of one cylinder at TDC and then turn the crankshaft anti-clockwise until the appropriate set of points is closed. Spring them open, and insert the cigarette paper. Slowly turn the rotor clockwise while gently pulling on the paper until it just frees. Note the position of the timing gauge, and then turn the crank further until the piston reaches TDC. This should be 3 mm beyond the point at which the paper freed

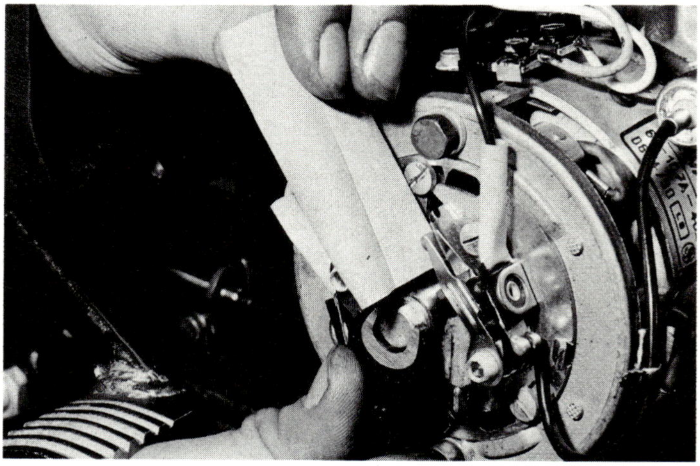

Except on very simple engines, where timing is adjusted by varying the gap between the contact-breaker points, the usual method is to free the backplate and rotate it to alter the point at which the spark occurs. Turning the plate against the direction of crankshaft rotation advances the ignition; turning it in the same direction as the crankshaft revolves retards it

With two sets of points on a two-piece backplate, there is a separate adjustment for each cylinder. To adjust the timing on the second cylinder, the two screws indicated are freed to allow the other half of the backplate to be turned as required

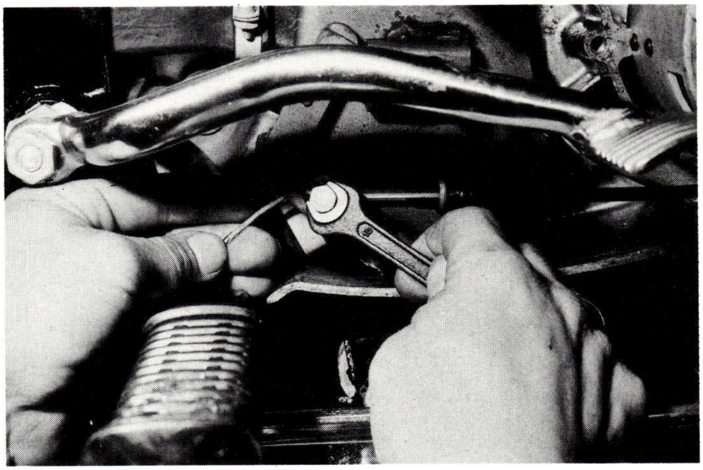

East European and Italian bikes tend to use solderless nipples on some cables, such as the clutch. The clutch adjuster is first screwed fully home, and then the bolt on the nipple is loosened to enable the cable to be pulled through. When the necessary play has been taken up, the cable is held while the nipple's bolt is retightened to hold the new adjustment. Final adjustment then takes place on the outer casing adjuster at the handlebar, or in the casing itself

The Jawa has a semi-automatic clutch whose linkage may need adjusting. With this, the solderless nipple is loosened, and left loose while the clutch adjusting screw is turned. When the bearing wheel at the end of the operating arm just rotates in the auto-clutch cam the cable slack is taken in, the nipple locked, and lever play adjusted to 2 mm

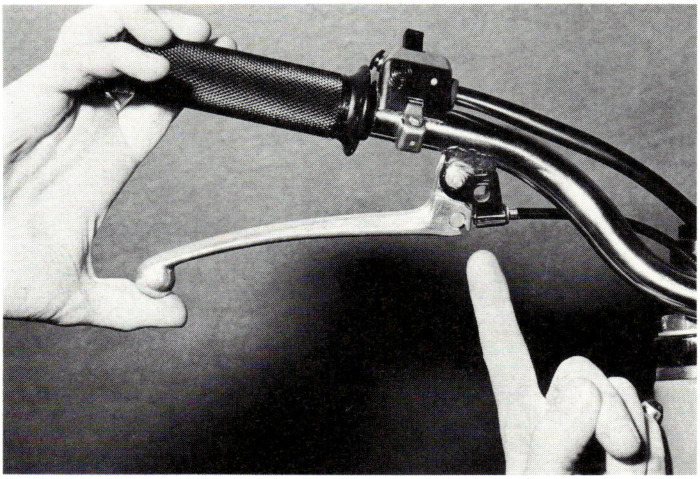

Lever play is specified in two ways in different handbooks. Generally, small amounts of play – up to 5 mm – will be between the lever and its abutment, as shown here. Greater play is measured at the ball end of the lever

Most chain-drive motorcycles have this type of draw-bolt chain adjustment, although there are exceptions – such as Ducati – which use an eccentric instead. After loosening the spindle nuts and the adjuster locknuts, the draw-bolts are turned one flat at a time on each side to pull the wheel backwards and so tension the chain. On the Jawa, the free play is measured by lifting the upper rubber gaiter containing the top run of the chain. Play at the tightest point – checked by rotating the wheel and testing at three or four different points on the chain run – should be 30 mm. On bikes without chaincases the play is checked on the lower run, and about 18 mm is the norm. After the chain tension has been set, it is advisable to check the wheel alignment by placing a plank edge-on against the wheels. It should touch both rims at two points

Some makers – Jawa among them – recommend frequent decokes of the silencing system and the head and ports. Silencer baffle tubes are removable for easy attention. This one is locked by a screw, and can be drifted away with a hammer and block of wood if it sticks. The best way to remove the carbon is to burn it off with a blow-torch, but soaking overnight in a weak acid such as ordinary malt vinegar will do the trick too

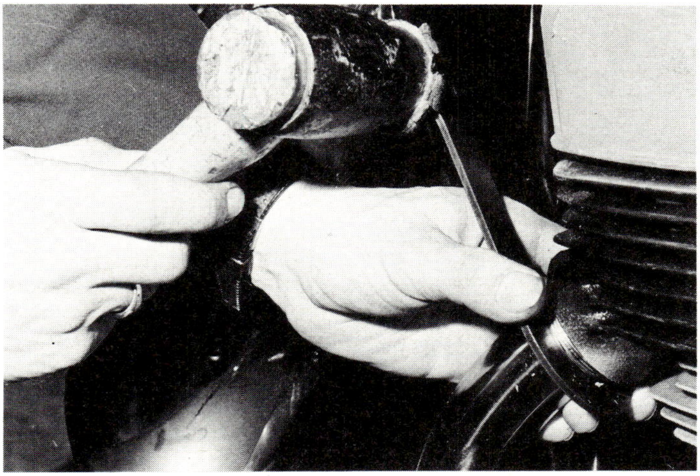

The Jawa is one of the easiest two-strokes to decoke, as it has separate heads and barrels. Start by removing the exhaust pipes. Here, they are held by a screwed-in ring. Variations include bolted-on flanges, or sprung stubs.

Any seals, such as this copper ring, must be refitted. If the exhaust system is faulty, a two-stroke will not develop its full power or give its proper economy

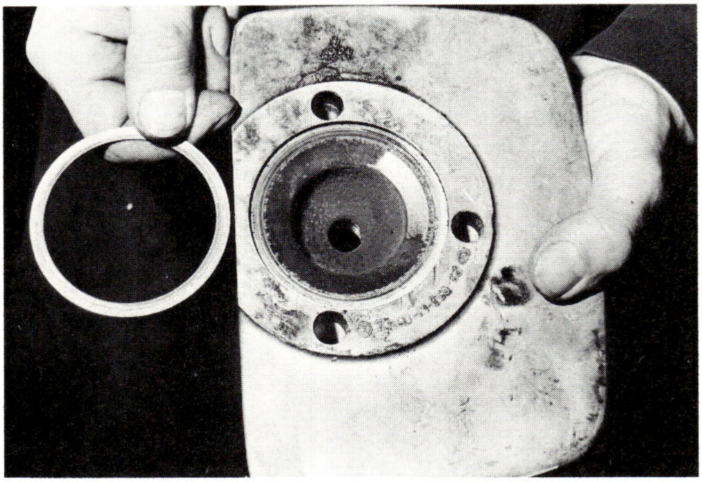

The most sensitive part of a two-stroke's combustion chamber is the area around the sparking plug. All carbon deposits must be removed – a piece of carbon becoming incandescent can cause pre-ignition. Renew gaskets such as this sealing ring, too

Set each piston in turn towards the bottom of its stroke and slide the barrel off its studs. Where a twin has a single barrel, set both pistons halfway down the bores

Check the piston rings for wear by removing them from the piston and inserting each in turn in the bore. Insert the piston, inverted, from below, and use it to square up the ring about 10 mm from the mouth of the barrel. Then check the ring gap with a feeler gauge. The reading should not be more than the maximum permissible gap quoted in the relevant manual

Air filters need periodic cleaning. Jawa recommend 1,500-mile intervals, with renewal of the dry element every 9,000 miles. Removal of two screws on the air filter cover allows it to be lifted out. It can be cleaned with a garage air line

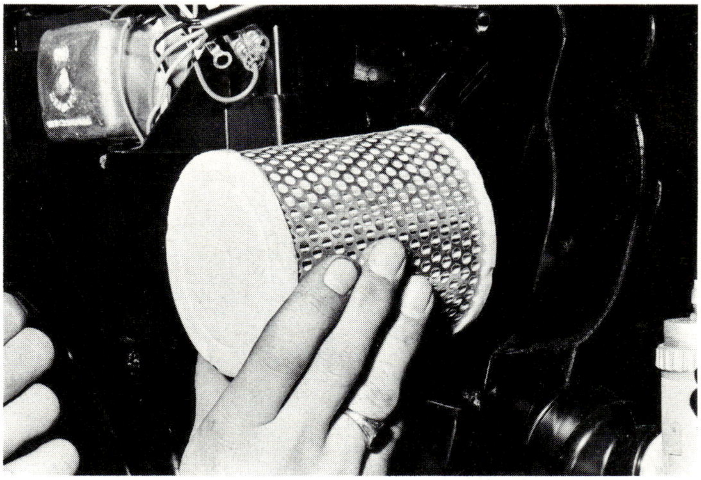

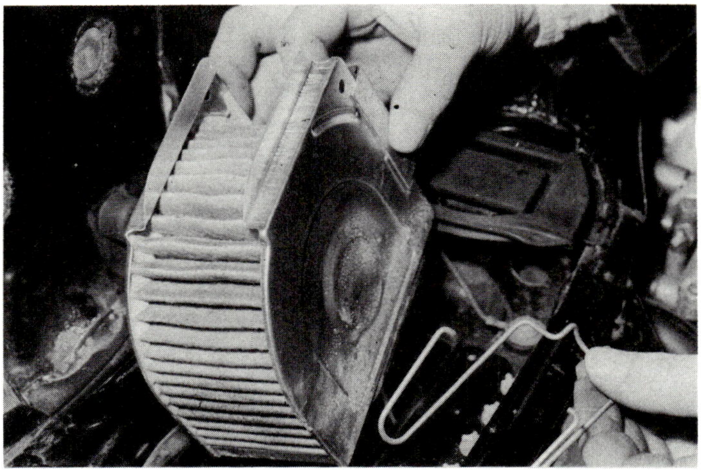

Variations on the routine maintenance theme.

Honda's CB400F dry air filter lifts out after releasing a spring clip. It is blown clear

The seemingly-similar filter on the Suzuki GS400 also lifts out – but . . .

. . . the foam plastic element is held by a spring, so that it can be removed to be washed in petrol, soaked in engine oil, and then re-inserted

On most Hondas valve clearances are still adjusted by screwed tappets on the rockers, reached through access holes in the cover

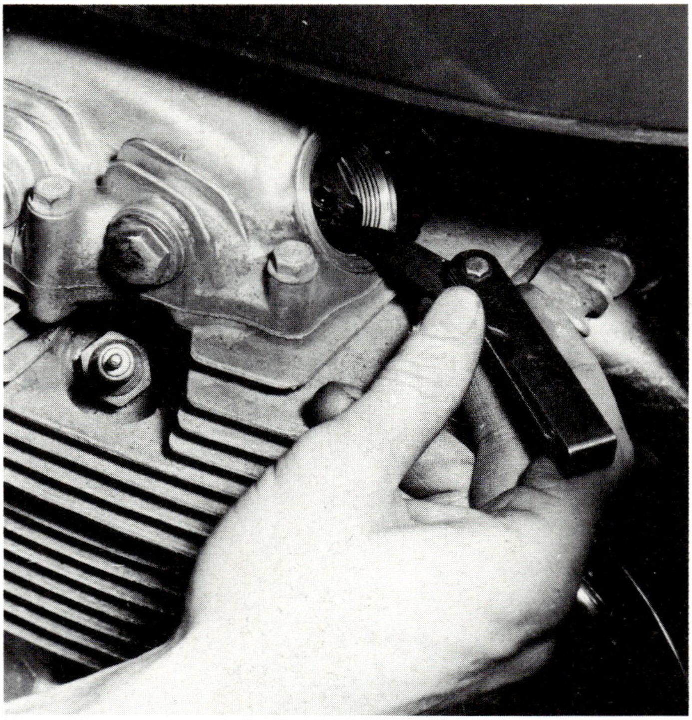

By contrast, the double ohc Suzuki 1000 employs shim adjustment. To lower the bucket tappet and allow the shims to be withdrawn for changing, the special bucket compressing tool shown here is used

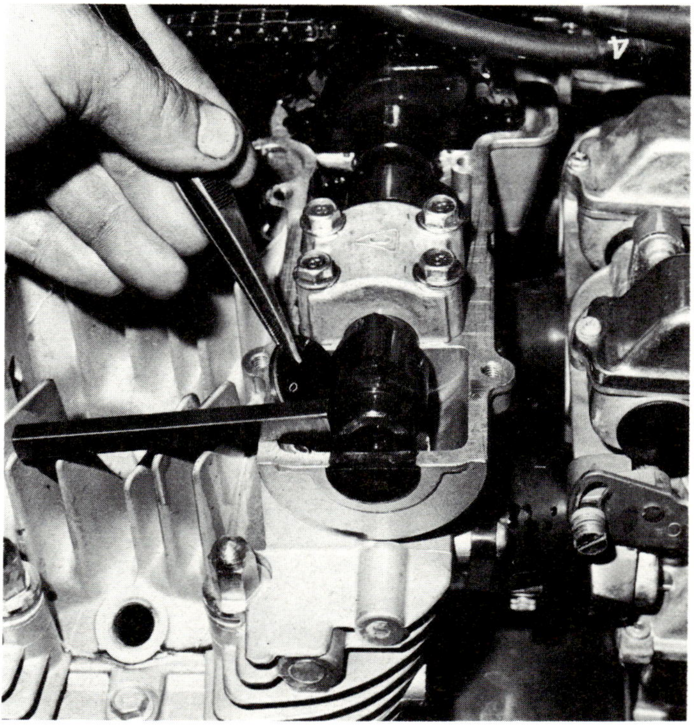

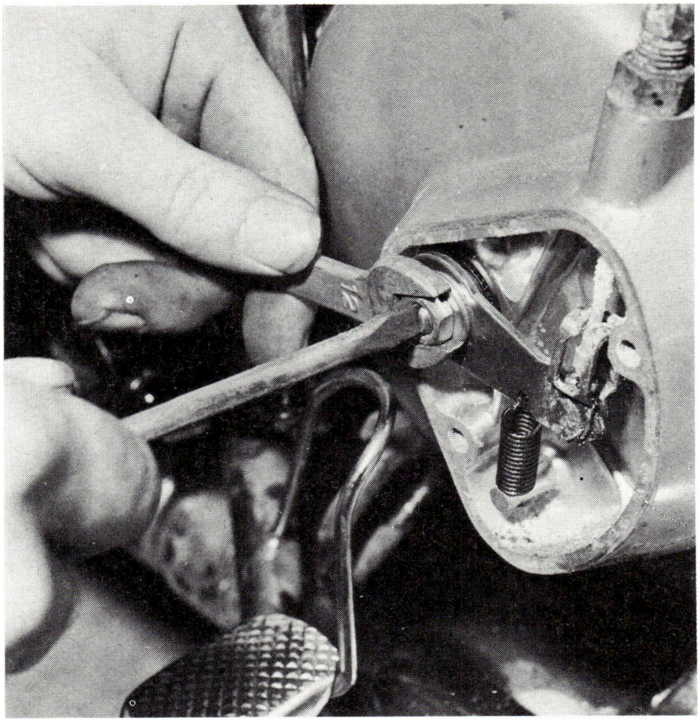

This type of clutch adjuster, common on Japanese bikes, uses a screw to set the clutch release, and a locknut to hold the setting

This Suzuki oil filter is set vertically into a housing in the sump

Typical Honda practice is to have a separate oil filter bowl bolted to the front of the engine, containing the renewable filter element and a by-pass valve

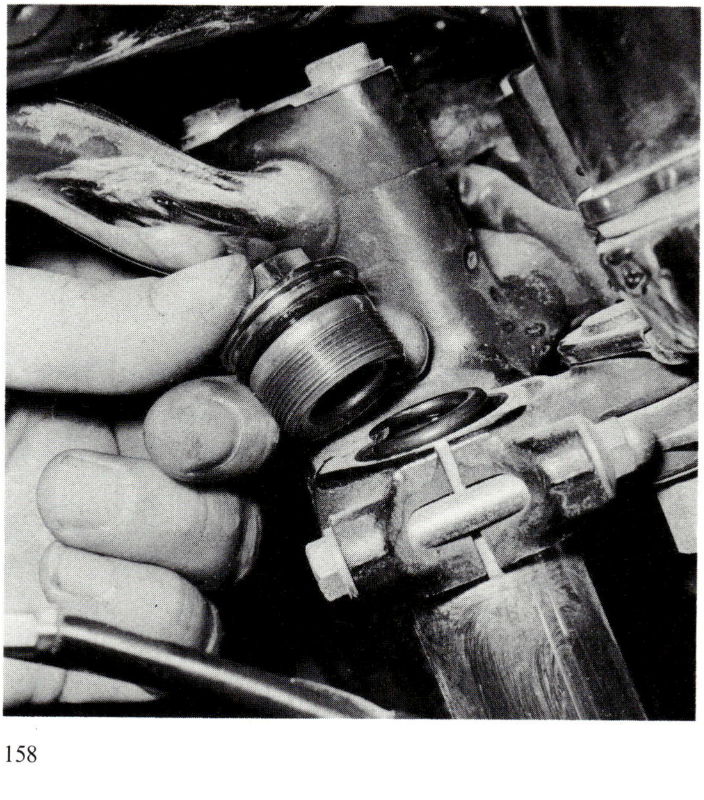

When the fork leg plug is removed on Ceriani-type forks, as on the Honda CB400F, the suspension spring slightly protrudes

Index